Copyright © 2016 by Ralph Eugene Tucker
All rights reserved.

Green Ivy Publishing
1 Lincoln Centre
18W140 Butterfield Road
Suite 1500
Oakbrook Terrace IL 60181-4843
www.greenivybooks.com

ISBN: 978-1-944680-38-1

To Harriette,

I will always rev. for your logical and plan... mind. Your smile is a gift. May it never dim. I pray that you and Michael will not only be blessed to see wonderful days together, but that you will continue to inspire others together. I pray that something in the pages of this book will bless you both as parents and leaders in the community

Love,
Ralph
February 12, 2016

Thugs in the Kingdom of Heaven

Calling Thugs and Saints

By Ralph Eugene Tucker

This book is dedicated to...

My son, Ralph William Tucker, whose passion, humor, wisdom, and thought-provoking conversations always challenge and inspire me.

And the students and staff at Lakeview School in Durham, North Carolina, who helped me to see the potential for greatness that lies in our thugs and wayward youth.

Table of Contents

Preface		IX
Chapter One	Thug Life	1
Chapter Two	Enter the Conversation	11
Chapter Three	Facing Ghosts	27
Chapter Four	Tight Places/Mean Faces	37
Chapter Five	Model of a Man	45
Chapter Six	Behind the Mask	55
Chapter Seven	A New Conviction	61
Chapter Eight	Self-Rule	77
Chapter Nine	Calling Moms and Dads	91
Chapter Ten	Calling Thugs and Saints	101

Preface

A man walked into a crowded church brandishing a 9-millimeter handgun. He had a bandana on his head, and his arms, neck, and face were tattooed. As he walked to the front of the church, gun in hand, he asked, "Who in here is willing to die for Jesus Christ?" Hearing no response and sensing the terror, he said, "If you are not willing to die for Jesus, I am going to give you a chance to get out of here alive." The choir section, the pulpit (preacher included), and the pews cleared with the exception of one elderly woman. As he approached her, he looked for signs of fear but found none. He sat down next to her, laid down his gun, and said, "Now tell me about this Jesus whom you are willing to die for and why." I am sure that he heard about a different Jesus from her than he would have from those who ran out of the church. I would love to have been privy to the conversation between that young man and the woman in the church because I am sure that they engaged in some meaningful conversation. I am sure that neither they nor the church were the same after that encounter.

He put his own life at risk many times as a gang member, but he wanted to talk to someone willing to die for a belief that was stronger than his and loyal to something greater than he had been. He had believed in something he was willing to die for, but not without his gun and, until now, not without his gang members. Here he met someone who was willing to die, without a gun and without her gang (who ran off and left her out of fear), for what she believed. Here, on this church pew, was an opportunity for a thug and a saint to have a meaningful conversation because fear had left the room.

I believe the heart of a true thug reaches the point of wanting to serve something greater, but the thug is not willing to follow someone they perceive to be weak, and weakness is always defined by fear. I also believe that every true saint reaches the point of wanting to do something greater for God but is often unwilling to take the leap of faith to rely on God's strength and direction. True thugs want to operate in a state of fearlessness, and true saints want to operate in a state of fearless love. When the counterfeit thugs and the counterfeit saints clear the room, the real thugs and the real saints can have a conversation in which they may find that they have more in common than they thought. Perhaps, through a dialogue between thugs and saints all over the world, we may see the manifestation of the Kingdom of Heaven. "Real recognizes real," and if we are going to be ready for the shift that is coming in our world, we are going to have to be real in every aspect of our lives and at every level of society.

I challenge every thug to come out from behind the gun and the gang, to meet the God who is great enough to bring gangs and nations to their knees and more powerful than any force that opposes them. I also challenge every Christian and every religious person to come out from behind their Bibles, churches, and religious creeds, to determine whether their faith is strong enough to stand the death test. When I have had honest interactions with thugs, without façade or pretense, often their respect for God was greater than that of some religion people who were strong in their profession but more fearful of people than of God. No matter which side you find yourself on, it seems that we are fast approaching the time of showdown where the fearful and unbelieving may have to come out of hiding.

Chapter One

Thug Life

At one time, the term thug was an insult even to thugs themselves. That was when 'thug' meant "a common criminal, who treats others violently and roughly, often for hire," as defined by Webster's dictionary. In a relatively short period, the term has gone from a negative label to one with positive appeal for a large segment of the population, around the world. Young men proudly call themselves thugs, and young women seem to be attracted to their thug persona. The term, made popular by rapper Tupac Shakur, whose album "Thug Life" sold millions of copies worldwide, became a badge of honor for many. According to the Urban Dictionary, Tupac defined thug as "someone who is going through struggles, has gone through struggles, and continues to live day by day with nothing for them. That person is a thug, and the life they are living is the thug life." His raw lyrics and his desire to be true to himself continue to inspire young gang members throughout the world from gangs in Brazil to youth in South Africa. While the "thug life" glamorizes criminal behavior, it is necessary to look at this criminal behavior worldwide and ask whether gang violence is an outgrowth of a society that has neglected its poor. Do our religious, economic, entertainment, political, and educational systems play a part in strengthening gang violence because so many youths around the world struggle to survive? Do these institutions provide the catalyst for the self-destructive behavior that plagues so many young people around the world and destroys so many communities?

In most major cities around the U.S., black on black crime has been a serious problem for many years. Now we tend to link most crimes in the inner city to gang violence. Whatever the source of the problem, we have growth in violence and homicide in our inner cities. While it is not all gang related, gang membership and gang violence have steadily increased all over the world. For families to lose sons and daughters to gangs and gang-related deaths has become the cost of living in many communities. Our youth must learn gang signs, handshakes, gang codes, and wear colors of identification for safe passage through the streets of their communities and in their schools just to survive. Once they have joined the gang, they must pledge allegiance to it even above their dedication to their own families. By some estimates, there are almost 1.5 million gang members in the United States today, in over 30,000 gangs. This increasing statistic is not only prevalent in the U.S., but gangs and gang violence is growing on every continent on earth with the exception of Antarctica.

So why the thug-life appeal and why has there been such a dramatic increase in gang membership in recent years? In order to answer these questions we must acknowledge the sociological and economic factors at play, but we must also look at the persons drawn into gang life or thuggish behaviors and the psychology of recruitment and retention. Throughout this book, when I use the term thug, I refer, in the narrow sense, to the thug on the local level in many communities and, in the broader sense, to a thug mentality found on all levels of our society throughout our world. In my mind, the only thing separating the common thug from those thugs who wear suits and titles is often whether or not they have the law on their side or how well they operate outside of the law. At bottom, it seems to be a question of having the power to acquire things, turf, people, and territory, and having the resources and resourcefulness to protect them. In order to acquire, and to protect what we have acquired, we need the strength of a group or organization, which is the reason why gangs form in the first place.

While there have been gangs dating back to the beginning of time, the worldwide proliferation in the past thirty years grew out of the Cripps and Bloods gangs in Los Angeles, California, in the early 1980s. Even the notorious MS-13 gang that is strong in many South American countries grew out of southern California as they responded to the need to protect themselves from the gangs there. According to Tookie Williams, the founder of the Crips, the gang was created to protect the neighborhood, not destroy it. Is it by accident that these gangs grew out of neighborhoods plagued by poverty and underemployment and where many of the public resources were not available? Is it reasonable to give a person a gun and a badge and ask them to protect and serve a neighborhood full of people they do not like? Then suggest that that community has the same benefits of public service as communities protected by those who like the people they serve? Even in the movie *Westside Story*, a love story involving the families of two rival gangs, we see the gangs reflecting the need for community protection due to the failure of the systems of government and society that should have protected them. It is easy to condemn gangs and gang members as being the cause of the breakdown and destruction of our communities, but how often do we look at the failure of our religious, economic, entertainment, political, and educational systems as the cause of gang development and growth?

Gang language and gang organization often mirrors the language and organization of human groups and human relationships throughout history. There is an order and chain of command just as every military organization has had throughout history. Initiation into the ranks of the loyal and trusted involves proving yourself loyal to the organization. This begins with nurturing a sense of belonging and family that fosters a feeling of safety inside the group and protection against any external threats or dangers. After all, everyone needs to feel protected. This feeling of family fostered by proof of 'blood' loyalty creates a sense of invincibility to any outside threat. This loyalty is established and strengthened by members undergoing initiation, often through fear of being ostracized or punished in the same manner or worse than that of an outsider. These are the same methods used to foster patriotism by nations and loyalty to military organizations throughout history as well. It is also a common tactic used by cults and even respected religious groups. In these organizations, secrecy and fear of reprisal produce loyalty, and traitors, snitches, informants, or spies receive the kiss of death. Traitors must die, "snitches get stitches," and informants and spies must hide or risk life, limb, and the lives of those they love.

We may be born self-centered and selfish, but we are not born thugs; that is an acquired malady. We are also not born to live in isolation from others. As social beings, the family, community, nation, and world we live in influence all aspects of our lives. The environment and the climate must be conducive to breed thugs on any level of society. Whether it is a street thug, entertainment thug, corporate thug, or religious thug, all grow out of an environment that implicitly or explicitly condones and supports thuggish behavior. In some ways, we allow room for some people to suspend or operate outside of the ethical boundaries of the larger community. Realistically, whether a thug wears a three-piece suit or a bandana and a hoodie, a thug is a thug. Whether the thug calls a board meeting in the conference room or a 'set' meeting in a schoolyard or abandoned building, the purpose is to make sure the thug comes out on top at the expense of others. The more widely accepted or marketed the justification, the easier it is to reach greater levels of thuggish behavior with little or no effect on their conscience.

The question often raised is whether art imitates life or life imitates art. I think it is safe to say that we learn from our environment as well as from those who nurture us. If our senses are flooded with trillions of terabytes of visual and audio information conditioning our minds daily, I believe it is safe to say that art influences our lives as much as, if not more than, our lives impact art. As I listen to students in school hallways and young men singing or rapping on the streets in every city I visit, I hear the repeated beat and lyrics of rappers, almost like a secret language among members of a secret society. The meaning of the lyrics could only be decoded with great effort and sometimes only by knowledge of the hip-hop culture out of which they came.

While working as a behavior support assistant at Lakeview School Therapeutic Learning Center for middle and high school students in Durham, North Carolina, I took students to the library to look for a biography to read and write a paper on for their class projects. As I assisted the students in their search, I ran across two copies of Ben Carson's *Gifted Hands*. I encouraged two of the sixth grade students to read it for their projects. To my surprise, both boys said that they were looking for a book on Tupac Shakur. What stumped me was that the year before, given the same assignment, a few of the high school boys also wanted to read about Tupac. I asked why this self-proclaimed thug had so much appeal to a generation of young black boys, men, women, and even white youth almost twenty years after his death. As I began to inquire, I found out that even some of my colleagues in education were under the influence of his thug appeal. Could this be a hybrid of W. E. B. Dubois' double-consciousness at work?

The shapers of the hip-hop culture seemed to be in a desperate fight to retain and regain a manhood threatened with extinction. On the other hand, perhaps they found a way to make money on the desperate hopes of a lost generation. Gangster rap, and its redefinition of manhood as expressed through a culture of violence may ironically be the result of some kamikaze attempt to save the manhood of a generation of young men, or an attempt to obtain a manhood that they never knew. While there has been a historical assault on the souls of black folks in America and throughout the world for hundreds of years, I have come to believe that this assault is merely a particular and politicized expression of the same assault that violently and pervasively divides communities and nations all over the world.

Some people have argued that America and Western civilization set out to subjugate and destroy the black man around the world. Whether by design, circumstance, or as a byproduct of power relations between nations in the world, black Americans and darker skinned people all over the world seem to be the most criminalized and impoverished peoples. My perspective grows out of my own experiences and observations of the world as a black man in the United States of America for over half a century, but I believe it will shed some light on the failed concept of manhood that affects us across racial and national boundaries, and which threatens to destroy our world.

I asked my son, who was thirty years old at the time, his thoughts of Tupac Shakur and the gangsta rappers. In his opinion:

> *They are searching for something and acting as though they have already found it. They are trying to find out how to be a man,*

but acting as though they are supermen. They need a new concept of what it means to be a man so they are constantly redefining themselves. The system that involves the music industry is working effectively to produce a concept that is going to be lucrative. The images of men they see in entertainment are often a joke and have no resemblance to the real world. The industry of hip-hop is a joke because the images portrayed by rappers are just images and the kids look at the image as real and try to re-create them. They cannot see behind the music. They do not know about their struggles and their journeys. Lil Wayne is intelligent, but everything that comes out of his mouth is industry approved. They are portraying an image that these kids are trying to emulate. He cannot sound too intelligent; if he does, his music will not sell. We need to unmask everyone behind a mask that deceives us from finding our true selves.

When a black man seeks knowledge about himself and arms himself to protect his community, they turn us on ourselves for cash. The drug trade in the inner city directly correlates with the movement to emancipate black manhood. The drug game, the prison system, and law enforcement go hand-in-hand, and there has to be an unsavory connection between them. Daddy, I know conspiracy theories are not provable, but you do not have to be a genius to see that black men make up the largest per capita population of the prisons and most of them are in there for crimes involving drugs or guns. How many black people do you know who own ships to bring drugs into this country? How many black people do you know who have gun-manufacturing companies or gun shops to provide so many illegal guns to the black communities all across this country? There are just too many unanswered questions, so it not only seems to be a conspiracy but a well-organized plan to destroy us and use us for the highest profit.

Tupac saw the curtain pulled back, and he was so distraught that he became depressed. He was dead before he died because he felt so helpless to change what he saw. It is almost as if he made Negro Spirituals for the next generation. Tupac takes you on a ride no matter what your situation is. These kids identify with his lyrics because they live with or have some association with his struggle. He has more money than you do, more women than you do, more drugs than you do—bombarded with images of sex, money, murder, and power, they try to live out the lyrics as reality or repeatedly seal them in their brains as fantasy.

We have to deprogram the young people and ourselves by exposing the system. We have to teach them about the branches of government and ask them to evaluate whether those branches are working for them or against them. At every level of society and government the question must be, "Is this working for me or against me?" Perhaps we can use hip-hop to re-educate because to listen to hip-hop, your mind has to work. Hip-hop is probably one of the most difficult genres to write, listen to, and interpret. While artists may not be aware of the names of the literary tools they are using, hip-hop employs alliteration, simile, rhyme, etc., and because the beat and the lyrics are repeated and well known throughout the community, it can become an effective educational tool. Even now, there are rappers who have a positive message. Nas the rapper's song "I know I Can" encourages listeners to believe in their ability to be what they want to become.

Black on black crime is rooted in racism. We did not just go from marching together in the sixties to shooting each other. We are used to being tricked, but historically we were more aware of the tricks played on us, and we knew how to trick back and how to trick ourselves into weathering the storms that we faced. Today we are not tricking anybody. Even churches need to establish a new brand. Churches may do better not to brand everything as a Christian event—let kids have fun and teach them. Kids are looking for acceptance. When people feel accepted they are more receptive.

Chapter Two

Enter the Conversation

As I listened to my son's passion, it seemed to echo so much of my own. Hope lies in the angry desperation that fills the air of the black community throughout the world. It is a hope that would die, if we could live without it. Fortunately, we cannot survive without our hope and the hope that has arisen generation after generation in spite of the conditions in our world that seem to be killing us. I remember the near-palpable anger and tension in the air as I grew up in Cleveland, Ohio, during the aftermath of the race riots of the late 1960s.

Finding productive ways to vent and talk about the problems and imagine solutions proved to be good for my friends and me. However, I discovered that when we congregated, whether in the park, a restaurant, or on the street corner, almost every other group perceived us as a threat. Depending on where we were, if we had a basketball or football in our hands, we were okay, but if we were having intense, meaningful conversation, others seemed intimidated. Even at the newspaper company where I worked while going to college and in each college I attended, the congregation of black men having a serious conversation aroused suspicion and fear. I knew at that point that there must be something powerful about black men talking seriously about anything that affected their well-being in the world.

I believe we can better understand who the real enemy is and better our world through dialogue and conversation. If we can heal the mind through conversation in a psychiatrist's or psychologist's office, can we not heal so much in our world by merely talking honestly and listening carefully to each other? As long as we are talking to each other there is less likelihood of us fighting, killing, or abandoning each other. In an attempt to understand why there was so much disparity between and within races and nations of peoples, I talked with co-workers, friends, fellow students, and anyone who was willing to listen and engage. Over forty years ago, I attempted to bring people of diverse backgrounds together to talk about ways to better our world and bridge the gap between races, cultures, and social classes. I invited friends, co-workers, classmates of various religions, races, and social classes to my parents' home to join in the conversation. My mother would fix desserts or refreshments, and my parents would often sit in and participate in the conversation, which would sometimes go on for two hours or more. Oftentimes our conversations engendered further conversations on the job and in the school environment. The conversations also enabled us to understand each other better, producing friendships and associations that have lasted over forty years.

I have endeavored to restart and keep the conversation going that began for me over forty years ago. I want to know why we cannot better our world without having to destroy or denigrate others in the process. Since this is a world for all of us, all of us should have a voice in the conversation. The problem of communication in our world is not a problem associated with one group but with the entire human race. Consequently, our lack of communication threatens the well-being of the entire world. The health of relationships, nations, groups and indeed the world, hinges on our ability to communicate with each other.

Healthy conversation requires open-mindedness and a willingness to listen to the other side's point of view. Emotions and personal feelings get in the way of hearing and often lead to defensiveness and anger. If a person cannot hear through the other person's anger and defensiveness without taking it personally, his or her own anger and defensiveness will get in the way of communication also. Sometimes one person's calm can settle another person down, but rage in response to rage not only makes communication impossible, it can also lead to violence and death. I believe most breakdowns in conversation and attempts to communicate occur when listening becomes defensive, leading to anger, which if not checked, can become irrational. When anger and defensiveness are out of control, it is difficult to understand the other person's position and even more difficult to rationally explain one's own.

When collective anger becomes personal, it is difficult to see the big picture because the person in front of you becomes the picture or embodiment of the whole problem and the target of your anger. I have seen this in effect when blacks talk about a societal problem, which they believe to be an injustice. As tempers rise, it becomes easy to blame "the white man" for almost anything. The same occurs on the flip side; when a crime has been committed, it is often easy for whites to say "a black man" probably did it. As time progressed, I too found myself in a place where my frustration with the collective problem became personal, and I began to vent my anger towards persons and groups rather than at the problem itself. I tried to say it was "the system" or the way "the system" was set up that caused us so much pain and injustice. No matter where you attribute the blame, it is still going to take fair-minded human beings to communicate and resolve problems.

Though many things have occurred in my life to challenge my hope that one day we would be able to talk to each other as human beings with love and wisdom, I have not lost hope; and my faith is stronger than ever that something miraculous is in the offing. Many have had the same hope and dreamed of better days ahead but did not see them. Langston Hughes wrote a poem asking, "What happens to a dream deferred?" Hope deferred is still hope. A dream does not always die with the death of the dreamer, but like the phoenix rising from the ashes, the seeds of dead dreamers arise in the hearts of new dreamers who refuse to let them die. Sometimes those seeds also pop up in unlikely places seeming to prove the old adage, "There is nothing more powerful than an idea whose time has come." Maya Angelou expressed this powerfully with her life and in a poem with the reiteration of the words "still I rise," and though she and Langston Hughes are no longer here in the struggle with us, their poetic and creative genius will continue to inspire generations.

The conversations that we need to have must been done with honesty, recognizing that death and life are in the power of our tongues. If we are to establish a new power dynamic, not based on how physically strong a person is, or how much money they have, or how many people are on their side, we must look at power from a new and uncommon perspective. Whether you believe the story of the tower of Babel found in Genesis chapter 11 in the Bible or not, their unity and their ability communicate clearly with one another enabled them to build with an eye and the potential to reach far beyond earth. When their conversation and communication was blocked, their unity and purpose was lost. For those who can see the connection, on the day of Pentecost in the book of the Acts of the Apostles in the Bible, the same God who confused our speech restored unity and communication. A new conversation began on that day, and it is still going on. It is this conversation that I invite you to enter, especially if you long for a deeper understanding of Jesus, who initiated the conversation.

I reach out to thugs with this invitation because I believe

they have an understanding of what it takes to be a soldier initiated through blood. If you are afraid to die for what you believe, you will not make the sacrifice that brings the power to unify. Jesus said, "Whoever will save his life will lose it, and whoever will lose his life for my sake and for the gospel will save it." (Mark 8:35) The question for the thug is simply whether or not Jesus is the one to lead them, and if so, what next? When I talk to men about Jesus, I refer to Him as being the most powerful man I have ever read about or encountered. I tell them that I am not talking about a wimp or weak man but a man among men, a man that even the toughest thug would have to respect. To operate as a thug, you have to operate in the currency of fear, but those who take on the character and spirit of Jesus operate in a spirit that is stronger than fear. If you join this conversation, you may discover that this is a powerful time of change on the earth. When the people came out of the upper room with God, they turned the world upside down. Somehow, the focus of the conversation changed down through the centuries as the Spirit of the conversation changed to a different power source. What better place to test this or see the power of God at work than in the thug world.

In the thug world, power comes by demanding respect, but Jesus never demanded respect, he merely commanded it with the power of his presence. His power was one over spirits, not over people. His power was the result of self-discipline and self-control, not of his control over people. His power came because of his obedience to God, not his stated belief in God. Respect from others in this world, and in the thug world, is very important, and battles are often fought for it. Even after fighting for power and respect, warriors will show respect to opposing warriors because a warrior respects a warrior's heart. The dynamics of power change, however, when there is no fear of loss and no fear of death. On this level, it is possible to establish a new paradigm of power in which love creates an atmosphere of mutual respect where fear is no longer the controlling currency. This level of respect acknowledges the other person as worthy of respect based on the simple fact that they are a fellow human being.

When I was a special education teacher at the main campus of the Lakeview Alternative School in Durham, NC, a school for students in grades six through twelve who had histories of chronic misbehavior and were suspended from their neighborhood schools, a young man walked into my classroom to see one of my students and simply sat down and began disrupting my classroom. Known to be gang affiliated, and known to intimidate students and teachers, he simply disregarded my presence. I observed him for a moment and then asked him to step out of my class. Out in the hallway I challenged him saying, "How is it that you feel you can come into my classroom and disrespect me and my class?" He said, "I don't know you, and I don't have to respect you. Respect is earned." I looked sternly into his eyes and said, "I don't know you either, but you don't have to earn my respect. I give it to you automatically." He stepped towards me with an intimidating gesture but paused when he saw no fear in my eyes. I showed him my open hands and said to him, "I know what these hands are capable of, and since I have no quarrel with you, I'm not trying to hurt you with them." I told him, "My power doesn't come from earning respect; my power comes from giving it. Every time I see you in this hallway, I speak to you and show you respect, and I will continue to do so because my power is not controlled by your response." Each time I saw the young man I spoke to him, and he began to speak and show respect, even asking, on occasion, if he could come into my classroom, which I allowed on the condition that he show respect to my classroom and everyone in it.

So many young men and innocent bystanders are hurt or killed over what seems, to so many people, to be something trivial or meaningless, but in the eyes of the offended it is a display of disrespect. For many youths respect or an idea of respect is a measure of their value and self-worth, and to violate that in any way is the highest insult. They may not have a father or mother who can instill in them a sense of dignity and self-worth apart from what other people think or say to them or about them. Personal power built upon what others think or say about us is power given or taken away by others. A simple act of disrespect can throw off our internal balance of power and cause us to do and say things we ordinarily would not. I believe it is our need and desire for personal power that causes us to look for it everywhere but inside ourselves.

We have looked for power through the barrel of a gun; parents have given their children martial arts training thinking it will make their children safe in a world of violence. Some look for protection from the police or the military; others look for security in money, wealth, and political power. But none of these things can help a person overcome fear. In fact, the belief that any or all of these things will keep us safe increases our fear of being without them, which makes us more insecure. As I began to think about this simple reality, I thought of the Bible verse "But God has not given us a spirit of fear, but of power, and of love, and of a sound mind" (2 Timothy 1:7). Movies, television shows, and real-life news reports show clearly that people are losing their minds trying to protect themselves and what they have through methods, means, and measures that depend on guns, money, politics, or physical strength. If fear is the driving force that causes us to feel threatened by others and to threaten the lives of others, then how could power, love, and a sound mind be a more powerful force of security? If fear is a spirit, it is going to take a more powerful spirit to overpower it. I have glimpsed the truth of the biblical statement, "There is no fear in love; but perfect love casts out fear: because fear has torment. He that lives in fear is not made perfect in love" (1 John 4:18). I have also experienced the torment of fear and the confusion of an unsound mind, and I have been blessed to experience the power of love and its ability to overcome fear. Fear comes with the territory of life, but love in its most powerful expression, gives life and is more powerful than fear and death.

While working with middle school students in the therapeutic learning center, I did an exercise to demonstrate how easily they could lose their power or self-control simply by what others said to them. I had two students come to the front of the room, and I would challenge one student to maintain his or her cool no matter what the other student said to them. With words alone, the second student was to see if they could make the first student lose his or her cool and cause them to lose their power and self-control. I whispered to the second student to say something simple about the first student that would allow the student to continue to be calm and emotionally collected, giving them a sense of control. Then, because I knew the students fairly well and was acquainted with those things that would trigger aggressive behavior, I would progressively give the second student things to say that I knew would cause the first student to lose his or her cool. As soon as the first student lost his or her cool, I would say to the student, "You lost your power over a few words; you let someone take away your power." The students became excited about the exercise. They volunteered repeatedly to see if they could keep from losing their power. Eventually I heard students saying to each other in the hallway or in the classroom, "Don't let them take your power" or "They took your power." The exercise generated great conversation among the students, and they asked questions and engaged in thought-provoking discussions about gaining and losing personal power. Once, when a near fight broke out over the exercise, a student asked me with tears in his eyes, "Mr. Tucker, what was I supposed to do? Was I supposed to just let him talk about my mother like that?"

Fear was the driving force behind most of the aggressive acts in the exercise, whether it is fear of losing face, fear of appearing weak, or fear of physical harm. Fear creates an atmosphere of anger, which often produces a fearful and aggressive response in return. I heard that dogs sense fear and will often bite in response to fear. As I look back on my life, I find that my most difficult struggles occurred in an atmosphere of fear. Fear causes procrastination and paralysis, which produces stress, which throws everything internally and externally out of balance. Consequently, I discovered that my greatest enemy was not procrastination or stress but fear. My greatest victories in life have been victories over fear. For each victory I had to face my fears, go where I was afraid to go, do what I was afraid to do, look at things inside and outside of myself that I was afraid to look at, and trust God to help me become more than I had ever been.

Rather than honestly facing our fears and overcoming them, we often cover our fears by feeding on the fears of others. In order to create a force field around ourselves, we act as if we are fearless by invoking fear in others. The problem with this is that the fearlessness can only remain strong in an atmosphere where they are creating the fear. If the tables turn, and someone else creates the fear, then those once fearless become the fearful ones. It seems to me that true fearlessness is not dependent on an atmosphere but on a state of heart.

On another occasion, while teaching at Lakeview School, a student who had already been in the court system and had charges pending at the time told me that he was an usher and sang in the choir at his church. Many of the students in our school had spent time in juvenile detention or the county jail, and some had or were facing felony charges. I taught in one of two states in the country where sixteen-year-olds are adults in the criminal justice system. When I asked this young man how it was possible for him to worship God on Sunday and be active in gang and thug behavior the rest of the week, he responded, "Real thugs go to church." I have wondered for many years why the church in general seemed powerless to influence the violence and killings in the streets in most of our major cities, especially when churches outnumber gas stations, police stations, hospitals, funeral homes, and barber shops.

I once heard a story about a storefront church, which doubled as a juke joint. A juke joint was similar to a nightclub with dancing, drinking, gambling, and the occasional problems that went along with men and women vying for attention and/or people drinking too much. As the story goes, there was a parakeet in the place which was left uncovered during the week but on Saturday nights, as they rearranged the furniture to set up for Sunday church service, the parakeet was put in a corner and covered up so that it would not disturb the Sunday worship service. In their haste one Saturday evening, as they set up for Sunday service, they only partially covered the parakeet's cage. On Sunday morning, as the people gathered for worship, the parakeet peeked under the partially covered cage and squawked, "Same old crowd." I believe thugs, partygoers, and the irreverent should go to church, however, I believe we have a problem when thugs cannot be distinguished from saints, or when both the thug and the saint live as though the power of evil is greater than the power of God.

Ultimately, we are going to have dialogue and discuss with ears to hear each other. In my second year in Seminary, I was the president of the Black Seminarian organization and a member of the student council. The student council, the Black Seminarian organization, and the Women's office jointly sponsored a forum to which we invited students from schools all over campus. In order to stimulate debate and lively but serious discussion, I suggested the forum topic, "Racism and Sexism: Dialogue or Destruction." The atmosphere was tense, the discussion was lively and volatile at times, and because of the buildup, the campus police were on hand to make sure that it was a peaceful forum. I was on the panel, and at one point in the discussion, a white male stood up and angrily made a statement to the effect that blacks did not own anything and that we did not have the power to change anything. I responded with calm assurance, "Listen, my friend, we are all in the same boat together, and if you think your end is going to float and our end is going to sink, you are in for a rude awakening."

I have gained so much understanding from dialogue and conversation. To take a few pages out of my previous book, Humpty Dumpty Back on the Wall:

> *I even had a classmate, who came to be a close friend, who steadfastly defended the Confederate cause and esteemed the history of the South. Perhaps it was our agreement to persistently dialogue, in spite of our disagreements, which enabled us to be friends, even to this day. While he and I talked about many subjects, from theology to eastern religions, he insisted on defending his Southern heritage. In a sense, he was defending his family that had its roots in the South for generations. For me there was no familial attachment to*

white southerners or to the Confederacy, so the Confederate system seemed evil to me as one that orchestrated the dehumanization of my ancestors. Through conversations with my friend, I came to understand how difficult it might have been for him to participate in the vilification of his great-grandparents, grandparents, and maybe even his parents for their participation in the system whose hallmark for me was the terrorizing, dehumanizing, and lynching of blacks. However, to accept any explanation for the crimes against humanity that occurred in Southern history seemed to lend credence to, or justify the notion of white superiority. At the time, I could not give any validation to those who were in any way part of, or who had in anyway helped to sustain one of the most repressive and cruel systems of racial segregation and discrimination.

It was during conversations with this friend and other white friends, Northern and Southern born, that I became aware of long-standing contentions between Northern and Southern whites. My Southern white friends would accuse Northern whites of being hypocritical and argue that many Northern whites were no more in favor of black liberation than Southern whites were, and that they practiced just as much discrimination as whites in the South, just in a different form. My Northern white friends could not understand how my Southern white friends could even begin to justify anything about the history of the South that involved slavery or Jim Crow. I began to understand that in order for my white Southern friends to accept this view of their history, they would have to admit that the people and the culture that they revered most had been fundamentally wrong in their dehumanization of blacks in America. The pride of the South would become the shame of the South if we nullified those aspects of Southern history that grew out of the institutions of slavery and Jim Crow. Perhaps the main and most devastating accomplishment that came out of the agreement made by President Rutherford B. Hayes to pull the troops out of the South in 1887 was the enabling of the resurgence of the "pride of the confederacy." In all fairness to my classmates, I cannot say that the differences in opinions were always along North/South lines. However, when it came to choosing allies in discussions, more often than not, the line of demarcation seemed to have, as its geographical equivalent, the Mason-Dixon Line. In my opinion, prejudice, segregation, and racism have besmirched American History. The attempted annihilation of the American Indian, the enslavement of those brought here from Africa with the subsequent Jim Crow segregation, the treatment of the Chinese in the westward movement, the treatment of the Japanese in World War II, and the initial refusal to receive and aid Jews who were victims of the Holocaust are evidence of this besmirching. In addition to this, many immigrants who came from Europe also faced prejudice and discrimination that caused tremendous suffering. Those groups that found a way to assimilate eventually escaped some of the mistreatment resulting from prejudice because of their differences.

The thing that troubled me most about these conversations was that the more I heard Southern and U.S. history being justified, the more I heard my own history invalidated. There just did not seem to be a way to affirm all of the histories in this country while simultaneously affirming the self-esteem of all parties involved. History, however we may interpret it, always has a blind side, which when acknowledged, gives us insight as to our connection to other groups and the human race as a whole. Everyone's history has stellar moments and shameful elements. When we can embrace the good and the bad in our own history and in other histories, then we enhance our own self-esteem as well as the self-esteem of others. As we embrace more and more histories as our own, we *realize that all of human history is our history, and we find an identity that embraces the whole of our society and our present day world. After all history, like the starting blocks for runners in a race, is a starting point, not the goal, of our journey.*

In Seminary, I learned to give voice to many ideas about religion and spirituality that I had not been able to articulate. The challenge I faced was to develop a new understanding of God and myself in the world. The requirement to use sex-inclusive language in our writing and speaking gave me a tremendous amount of insight into just how much language defines who we are in the world. The constant reminder to be gender inclusive in my language opened my eyes as to just how male oriented our world is and how we perpetuate that through something as seemingly innocuous as our use of male personal pronouns to the exclusion of female pronouns when speaking in general. Power relationships in the world are traditionally gender-structured relationships, and women were at one time legally on the same level as property or livestock and still are in some places in the world.

While in Seminary, I also had a number of friends and associates from a cross section of academic disciplines and a number of different nationalities, e.g., Zaire, Uganda, Nigeria, and China. I benefited greatly from these friendships and the friendships with my black and white American friends. Our conversations were always stimulating and enlightening. I believe these conversations helped to broaden my worldview and my sense of being a citizen of the world.

The fact of the matter is that if we cannot hear and understand each other, no matter where we are on earth, we will wind up killing each other and destroying the planet. I recall watching one of the

Mad Max films in which the characters played by Tina Turner and Mel Gibson were fighting on opposite sides, and in the end of the fighting, they were the only two left on the battlefield. As both lay dying, with no other human life around them, they reached out to touch each other's hands. Let us not come to the hour of death to realize that "out of one blood God created all of us to dwell on the face of the earth." We must keep the conversation going no matter how angry we become or how difficult it is to hear the other person's point of view, but we must be in the conversation, and we must face our personal and collective histories with honesty.

Chapter Three

Facing Ghosts

Perhaps our fatal flaw as human beings is that we often forget our own mistakes and shortcomings as we look at the mistakes and shortcomings of others. A pastor said in his sermon, "Many of us might have gone to jail if arrested for some of the things we had done in our lives." In fact, some in the congregation had done time in jail or prison. Perhaps it makes us feel better about ourselves when we can say that we are not as bad as someone else; then we become quick to judge others and offer excuses for our own behavior. The more people I meet, the more I become aware of the fact that so many of us have had some dark and shadowy places in our lives. Like family secrets, whether publicly exposed or hidden, we all have something in our lives that have, or could have, brought us public shame or embarrassment.

Certainly, I could have spent time in jail if arrested for things I did when I was a teenager. While there may be no explanation for the twists of fate that occur in our lives, if we are honest with ourselves, we must say that none of us have been so perfect that we didn't need someone to look beyond our mistakes, failures, and shortcomings in order for us to survive. It would be an unbearable curse, and ultimately a death sentence, to feel judged every moment of our lives. With no hope of redemption or restoration, many people live in, and create for others, a literal hell on earth. Forgiveness and a process of restoration can break the curse and free all of us from the condemnation of judgment and its crippling guilt.

Thieves convince themselves that they are entitled to what they steal or that their wellbeing is dependent upon it. In the beginning, questions of right or wrong and legal or illegal may be considered, but after being convinced their survival depends upon their ability to steal or become involved in illegal or immoral activity, these questions become less and less important. Whatever the case may be, when the desire for what we do not have becomes stronger than our moral compass, it becomes easy to steal, lie, and manipulate in order to get what we want. We then must justify our behavior in order to live with ourselves, so we may say, "I am entitled to have nice things" or "They will never miss the little bit I take" or "They didn't work for it, and I deserve it as much as they do." The list of how we justify our poor behavior can go on. In order to set things right, we must face and tell the truth about ourselves.

Between the ages of sixteen and eighteen, I had a job and I became a thief. While in high school, I was cutting class with a friend who had a car. As we left the school and got to his car, he found that his battery was dead. He went to another car parked on the street, lifted the hood, exchanged batteries, and we drove off. When I found myself stuck one night with a dead battery at my girlfriend's house, I walked around the corner and down the street looking for a car that would be an easy target for a battery. It was a very cold night, but I saw a house with a well-lit backyard, so I eased up the driveway, stole the battery, and returned to my car. The same friend that showed me how to steal a car battery also introduced me to shoplifting.

For a short period, I became adept at stealing whatever I needed for my car from discount stores or any clothes that I wanted to wear from the finer department stores. The Bible says that "Time and chance happens to all of us," and my friend who taught me the ropes of stealing happened to get caught. I am sure that his arrest and other factors coming together in my life served as a wake-up call for me. Like the perfect storm, things began to come together that caused me to evaluate the direction my life was going and to change. As the Psalmist said in the scriptures, "I thought on my ways and turned my feet unto thy testimonies" (Psalm 119:59).

One of the things that helped me to mature was a scare that I had gotten my girlfriend pregnant. Perhaps because my father worked hard to provide for his family, I immediately began making plans to marry her and to seek full-time employment to take care of my responsibilities. Although it turned out to be a false alarm, it sobered me up to the consequences of sexual pleasure and the responsibilities of manhood. Even as I think about that period in my life, I recall a debate that my first wife and I had in college, which drew in the entire class on one side or the other of our debate. We were taking a philosophy course entitled Deductive Logic. I contended that logic and reason were stronger and more powerful than emotions, and she contended that emotions were stronger than logic. Perhaps at that time I was struggling, with some degree of success, to master my emotions by making wise and calculated decisions. I believe we both received an 'A' in the course, but I have revisited that debate repeatedly in my life, more often than not, conceding that my emotions overruled my logical mind. It is funny how experience can radically change the way we think.

Another thing that helped me face the possibility of real-world consequences was carrying a gun with no ammunition in it. My friends and I were going out one night, and one of them lived with his uncle who owned a gun. His uncle was away so he took the gun, but he could not find the bullets. We were in situations that night that were potentially volatile, and I realized that if there were bullets in the gun I had in my belt, I would have shot someone if it had come down to it.

It was then that I realized that talking your way out of a bad situation, or not saying anything at all, was better than killing someone or dying because of pride. I felt so unsafe with the gun with no bullets, and later I learned that I felt safer with no gun at all because I did not like the thought of what I was capable of with a loaded gun in a bad situation. It was so easy to hide behind the power of the gun because it made me feel invincible, as if I could face any challenge to my manhood.

Oddly enough, another thing that helped to bring about a change in the way I viewed the world was watching the movie, *The Exorcist*, at the age of eighteen. I do not know why, but that movie literally terrified me. I had nightmares and could not sleep well for a number of days. Finally, I decided to face my fears, so I decided to lay awake and invite whatever spirits or demons were present to show themselves. Lying there in the darkness, I believe I saw glimpses of both demonic and angelic images. Perhaps it was my imagination, but it really did not matter because I was amazed at how much peace I felt as I continued to wait. Although the movie left me feeling that the demonic forces in our world were indeed powerful, I found in the darkness the comfort of a presence that was more powerful than the greatest forces of evil that I could conceive of in my mind. Over forty years later, I have looked into the darkness many times and have experienced its overwhelming threat, sometimes in ways that paralleled scenes from *The Exorcist*, and I am convinced more now than I was then of the presence and power of God.

I still look into the darkness and continually discover aspects of light that I have not seen before. Sometimes sitting in meditation and prayer, I discover light in the darkness both emanating from within me and present around me. The more I am aware of my own light, the more I appreciate and respect the light I see in others. I wonder how many times we have missed opportunities to bring beauty to the world because we did not realize that there is a light in us that, when united with the light of others, can light up the world. There have been times that the light of others has helped my light to shine brighter and times when my light helped others to shine brighter. Perhaps it is only by facing and challenging our own darkness that we can reveal the light and dispel some of the darkness in the world. Sometimes even when we let our light shine, we do it from the shadows as if we are afraid of the darkness robbing us of our light. On the other hand, could it be as Marianne Williamson said poetically in *A Return to Love: Reflections on the Principles of a Course in Miracles*:

Our Deepest Fear

Our deepest fear is not that we are inadequate.

Our deepest fear is that we are powerful beyond measure.

It is our light, not our darkness that most frightens us.

We ask ourselves, who am I to be brilliant, gorgeous, talented, fabulous?

Actually, who are you *not* to be?

You are a child of God.

Your playing small does not serve the world.

There is nothing enlightened about shrinking so that other people won't feel insecure around you.

We are all meant to shine, as children do.

We were born to make manifest the glory of God that is within us.

It is not just in some of us; it is in everyone.

And as we let our own light shine,

we unconsciously give other people permission to do the same.

As we are liberated from our own fear,

our presence automatically liberates others.

I believe there are so many lights hidden by shame, fear, anger, guilt, ignorance, or any number of blockers that have caused people who were born to be stars to appear as black holes. In every major religion or spiritual movement the pilgrim always begins flawed, and then learns life lessons that produce growth and development. In our society we often punish, destroy, embarrass, and shame the bad people and label as a bad person anyone who does not believe as we believe. Somehow, we must reprogram our world to affirm the good in the bad people and acknowledge the bad in the good people so that we can turn criminals into heroes, and those who may not believe as we believe into allies. At this stage in human history, we must grow up fast and change quickly in order to save the lives of our children who are more fearful, violent, and disillusioned than ever. A clarion call goes out to the nations and peoples of the world to come out of the darkness of division and separation into the light of unity that recognizes that "[God] made of one blood all nations of [people] for to dwell on all the face of the earth…" (Acts 17:26). As we answer this call, we become the people who will bring about transformation in the earth. I believe God is recruiting an army of dedicated soldiers who are willing to learn from God and who are willing to dedicate their lives to fulfilling the mission that God has assigned for this appointed time. I believe this army includes people from all nations, races, religions, and classes of people, and that God is calling witnesses from the thug populations from all over the world to recognize that they may be called to be an integral part of God's present work on earth. The network of thugs throughout the world today may make it possible for the message to go global because the conditions out of which gangs are born are the same all over the world. Criminal organizations throughout the world with so much in common may be a vehicle God can use to complete the transformation of the kingdoms of this world into the kingdom prepared for us before the foundation of the world. Ultimately, they have no allegiance to a nation and operate outside the laws of the land. Their power operates on all levels of society ranging from those who seem to be above the law to those who have long rap sheets as outlaws.

Could God be calling thugs into the Kingdom of Heaven at this time so that it may become clear to all of us that, without the grace of God, there is no difference between us? The anger in the outcast outlaws throughout the world and their tendency to gravitate towards violence and group protection may indeed work for good in the end. Although the struggle to be accepted and safe in their world were struggles faced by every generation, the magnitude of the challenge for young men and women around the world today is unique to the present time. We find evidence of this in the thousands of young people fleeing from South and Central America to escape from gang violence and gang rule. However, we also find evidence in the fear that causes millions to join gangs and to do things that destroy the framework of our society. I hope this book will inspire some on both sides to imagine and realize their untapped power and potential for good. Lest I leave the impression that I write simply to the street thugs of the world, I believe the greater appeal is to that place in all of us where there is no difference between "them" and "us." As we see "us" in "them" and "them" in "us" we will be careful in even our smallest actions to heal and not wound, so that we are not destroying what we could have healed (Hebrews 12:13). As we face ourselves more honestly, looking at our failures, near failures, hidden thoughts, and successes, we can make a difference in the lives of so many others and become a positive force for change in our world. It is my hope that those readers, for whom fate has been kind and for whom divine grace is extended, will reach others by demonstrating how change and transformation can come to our world as we are changed and transformed ourselves.

We need radical change and nothing short of the miraculous in these difficult times. Even more than that, we need courageous people who are not afraid to die for the Kingdom of Heaven. In addition to poverty and disease, we seem to be on the verge of self-destruction by wars and the threat of war, the present danger of nuclear destruction, and armies of thugs who have created an atmosphere of fear and terror in local communities throughout the world. As sunlight turns night into day, I am convinced that God grants us mercy and empowers us, and the impending darkness that seems to be growing around us will ultimately be no match for the light of God within us. A thousand people of goodwill will strengthen the fabric of a society; however, the same good people, overcome by fear, becoming selfish and self-protective in times of trouble, can destroy that same society. Alternatively, a thousand people who have been antisocial and selfish, with a new spirit and moved by fearless love, can turn the world upside down and become an anchor of divine stability in times of chaos and confusion. It is time for a demonstration of God's power operating in us and in our world to prove what so many of us declare in our personal belief systems. If we believe that good is more powerful than evil, then we have a stage set before us every day on which we can demonstrate the realness of this power. As we approach a time of testing, it is time for us to let our lights shine bright enough to dispel the darkness that threatens our world. As thugs, thieves, liars, cheaters, haters, and miserable folks begin to face the ghosts of their past and yield to the Spirit of God, a disruption will occur in the status quo caused by a desire for peace on earth and goodwill towards all human beings. While this will surely expose all of us who benefit directly or indirectly from the oppression of the poor, our exposure can be our redemption. If we are honest, we may discover that money and material things have been more important to us than God or people. I believe that God is presently preparing a network of unlikely foot soldiers worldwide that, when mobilized, will surprise even the most religious of us. This network, like that of the criminal world, must encompass those on every level of society as God has held many in reserve for such a time as this.

Chapter Four

Tight Places/Mean Faces

My one major encounter with the police occurred when I was in the throes of a nervous breakdown. I went to a hotel in downtown Newark, New Jersey, to get some rest from the stresses that were overwhelming me at the time. As I was going into the hotel, I ran into four young black men. We began to talk to about their future as black men in America and the potential that I saw in them. They seemed to be interested in the discussion, so I invited them up to my room to continue the conversation. At one point, I went into the bathroom, and when I came out my car keys and my car were gone! I decided to get some rest and worry about it the next day.

No one knew where I was, so I decided to call my wife and let her know that I was okay and that I would see her the next day. Although I was careful not to say where I was, somehow in her worrying about me, she was able to find out. The next thing I knew, two of the elders from my church were knocking on the hotel room door. I told them that I simply wanted to rest and that I did not want to be disturbed. They insisted on knocking and trying to persuade me to open the door. The next thing I knew, the hotel manager called my room and asked me to leave, so I told the hotel manager that I had paid for the room and that I should have the right to my privacy.

When I saw a police officer through the peephole, I realized in my justifiable or unjustifiable paranoia that my life could be in danger. In order to bring attention from the outside, I started throwing things, including my clothes and shoes, out of the window and hollering for help. For some reason, I felt like I had to build a barricade. I took the mirror off the dresser and positioned it between the bedroom and the door, and I took a lamp, put it in front of the mirror, and positioned myself in the bathroom off the hallway between the mirror and the door to the room. I knew that they would cut the electrical power to the room, so I took the electrical plate off the light switch in the bathroom, disconnected the wires, and connected the wires directly to the lamp. As they were trying to get the passkey to get into the room, I quickly positioned myself in the bathroom, and as they opened the door, they turned off the power to the room.

    I still had power and with the light shining on the mirror, I could see them, but they could not see me. I saw several police officers at the door and in the hallway, and I said to them, "I think that's far enough. I paid for this room and no one can explain to me why I'm being asked to leave." Then I said, "President Reagan is not prepared to deal with what I have in here." The bomb squad was there and a negotiator was there to talk to me. I told him that I would not talk until I could talk to my lawyer. There was a lawyer (a black American) whose wife was a member of our church. I gave them his name and they sent someone to the courthouse where he was in session and brought him to the hotel. When I saw that he was shaking like a leaf, I told him to leave because he was scared and could not help me.

    It was just the negotiator and me and my belief that God had not abandoned me. Being aware of every movement at the entrance door and the subtle tests by the negotiator, I held them at bay for more than three hours until the negotiator convinced me that I could trust him. The negotiator was a white Italian American police officer. One may not think that it matters, but of all the police officers that were there, black and white, I somehow felt that I could trust him, even in view of what I heard from some of the other officers. As he tried to reassure me, I told him that I came into the hotel with my dignity intact and that I would like to leave in the same way. I told him that I would like to walk out with my clothes and shoes on just as I had arrived. I asked him if he would send someone downstairs to the front of the hotel to gather my clothes and shoes that I had thrown out of the window, and he said that he would.

As I surrendered, eight to ten police officers entered the room, some of whom seemed to be itching to get their hands on me. I looked at the negotiator and said, "You gave me your word." He sent officers downstairs to get my clothes, and as I got dressed, I realized that one shoe was missing. I looked at him again and said, "You gave me your word that I would walk out of here with my dignity intact." When I said that, I heard a tall white police officer say, "Just throw the nigger to the ground." The negotiator put his hand up to the officer and said, "Send someone down to look for his other shoe."

As I put on my shoes, and finished dressing, I noticed that even the black officers looked very nervous. Looking back on that situation, even having been in an altered state of mind, I realize that God was not only with me, but I believe He gave me wisdom and a strategy because the result could have been devastatingly different. I thank God that I am here today and that the dream of making a positive contribution to God's Kingdom on earth has not died.

I was eight years old at the time of John F. Kennedy's assassination. I was ten years old at the time of Malcolm X's assassination. I was thirteen years old at the time of the assassinations of Martin Luther King, Jr. and Robert F. Kennedy. They killed the dreamers who dared to dream that society could make a grand shift to elevate its poor and disenfranchised. Yet these dreamers knew that death was an imminent possibility, and in some cases a certainty, if they continued to arouse the hopes of the impoverished masses of all races and nationalities. What makes a dream stronger than the thirst for life in the dreamer? What makes a dream powerful enough to cause the dreamer to sacrifice his or her life with the belief that the dream will live on and spring forth into life? As dreamers continue to arise around the world, the dream will spring into reality. As long as only the most courageous become carriers of the dream, the dream will die with the dreamer. Instead of a pyramid-style leadership where the head can be cut off and kill the movement, we need an ameba-style leadership where there is no head to be cut off (at least no earthy head). An ameba is a single cell organism, which has no head, or foot. Anywhere it is cut simply grows back. An ameba-style leadership inspires every person to be a leader just as courageous and dedicated as everyone else. The death of one leaves no void because everyone is equipped to pick up the banner and fulfill the dream. Only soldiers who are not afraid to die can accomplish this kind of uninterrupted progression. As one protester held a sign in South Africa against apartheid, which said, "They can't kill us all," we must be willing to sacrifice ourselves for the Kingdom of God. One thing the Thug Nation has that is often lacking in religious organizations is that they are more willing to die for their cause. With a change of allegiance from self-promotion to an allegiance to God, they are better prepared for the Kingdom of Heaven. As Jesus said, "Whoever will save his life will lose it and whoever will lose his life for my sake and for the gospel will save it" (Mark 8:35).

The quest for a society where people live in honor and fairness with one another is as old as the human race itself. It is the stated desire of every form of government and every religion as far back as Hammurabi's code and the Mosaic Law. Whether it is a democracy, a dictatorship, or a communistic state, the stated reason for government to exist is to operate for the highest good of the people. Whether they do that or not, their manifestos, constitutions, and military decrees have the stated intent of maintaining an order that produces the greatest good, given our limitations as human beings. Yet with all of our intelligence, we have not been able to establish this utopian society eliminating poverty for millions of people. John Mayer expresses the frustration of those who dream of a just and fair society in the words of the following song:

>Waiting On The World To Change
>Me and all my friends
>We're all misunderstood
>They say we stand for nothing and
>There's no way we ever could
>
>Now we see everything that's going wrong
>With the world and those who lead it
>We just feel like we don't have the means
>To rise above and beat it
>
>So we keep waiting
>Waiting on the world to change
>We keep on waiting
>Waiting on the world to change

Generations have been waiting for the world to change. In my lifetime, I have seen the rising hopes of a generation dashed, rekindled, and dashed again. Some of us have become doomsday purveyors and some of us continue to believe that positive change will come in our lifetime that will liberate the poor and downtrodden peoples of the world. In the words of another popular song written by Billy Joel:

> We didn't start the fire
>
> It was always burning
>
> Since the world's been turning…
>
> No, we didn't light it,
>
> But we tried to fight it.

Like so many others, I live with the belief that we will have a social and moral awakening before the world ends. I believe that a new understanding of "Thy kingdom come, Thy will be done, on earth as it is in heaven" must occur in the world before the consummation of the ages, Armageddon, or the Lord Jesus Christ's return. For years, I have declared that, before this world can be saved, liberation has to come to the doorsteps of black America, and I believe that the de-valuation of black life in the United States is about to come to a head like a pimple that is ready to burst. The burst has to occur and the poison released from the system. Since the United States has been the greatest purveyor of oppression for economic gain, it makes sense that the people whose slave labor made America great and the world rich should be the recipients of healing to begin the restoration of the Kingdom of God on earth.

Black Americans may qualify as perhaps the most despised group of people on earth. People of every nationality come to the United States of America, the greatest nation on earth by many standards, and are often given higher esteem and greater respect than black Americans who are the progeny of African slaves. Even in 2015, the poorest and most uneducated white people may receive higher esteem simply because of their race than black people who are more highly educated and more financially well off. This scenario, repeated throughout the world with people of similar and different defining characteristics, is a major cause of rebellion and hatred for the United States.

The poorest people in the world provide the labor and live in settings of great wealth held by a few. In many nations, the resources of the country provide great wealth for people in other parts of the world when the people of the country are left impoverished, e.g., blood diamonds coming out of Angola. In these nations, natural resources or labor, as in the case of slave and Jim Crow labor in America, supported a lifestyle for a few maintained with laws that insured that nothing would block the flow of wealth. Black codes in the United States and similar laws in South Africa, Brazil, and all over the world created a system in which generations of young men and women died or spent long sentences in jail to protect the wealth of wealthy families and wealthy nations. The trickle down through time is that, even when slavery ends and the blood diamonds are exposed, new methods arise to make sure that wealth and privilege remains intact for those families and nations that benefitted from the historic oppression of millions of people.

Communities and nations all over the world are suffering today because of unbelievable historical and present-day policies and practices fueled by greed. We know that not all wealth acquired in the world was the result of greed without regard for human life. Nevertheless, there is a historical trail of greed which created the present-day conditions of poverty for so many communities around the world that have become the breeding grounds for thugs all over the world. These are the communities today in almost every nation whose children see few options for success or survival outside of gang involvement. This puts them in the category of "the last" qualifying them for the "last that shall be first." Being "the first" comes with a great price and a great sacrifice if we analyze the context and intent of Jesus' statement, "The last shall be first, and the first shall be last" (Matthew 20:16). When God makes the last first and the first last, it is not so that they will be glorified as a great people but that God may be glorified as a great God who can create and remake a great people. It has to be a people through whom all nations of the world are blessed. God says in scripture, "The foolish things of the world are chosen to confound the wise, and the weak things of the world to confound the things that are mighty, and the base things of the world and the things that are despised, hath God chosen. Yes, and things which are not, to bring to nothing things which are: that no flesh should glory in His presence" (1 Corinthians 1:27-29). According to this vision, even the most despised and criminalized can become the light of the world and a beacon for lost souls everywhere. In order for this to happen, we need a radical makeover as human beings on this planet. Like the World Wide Web, a network of people is already in place for sudden change to take place. This will require a new understanding of manhood for men worldwide and with the redefinition of manhood comes the redefinition of humanity.

Chapter Five

Model of a Man

I heard a story about a Papa bear that was walking along the road with his son teaching him about life. As they walked along the Papa bear told his son to make sure to watch out for the man. The young cub asked his father, "What is a man?" About that time, he saw an old man coming down the road and he asked his father, "Is that a man?" His father replied, "No, that used to be a man." As they walked along, he saw a young boy coming down the road and he asked his father, "Is that a man?" His father said, "No, he is going to be a man." As they traveled a little further, he heard the click of a double-barreled shotgun, and as the man raised the gun to shoot, the Papa bear said to his son, "Run, son, that's a man."

How do we define manhood? Does firepower define a man? When I was growing up in the 1960s, television portrayed manhood in cowboys played by actors like John Wayne and Clint Eastwood. The fastest gun was always the hero, and manhood was often determined through the power of the gun. The most popular shows on television were Westerns that showed how white men with guns conquered the western territories of the United States. Even benevolent men like Ben Cartwright in the television show Bonanza possessed his land by the power of the gun, and his family maintained their power through their ability to outshoot the "bad guys" and the Indians. The Lone Ranger had a Native American named Tonto as his sidekick who helped to legitimize the white males with the guns who took, by force, land once owned by Native Americans.

One of my favorite toys growing up was my gun and

holster. Playing Cowboys and Indians and having imaginary gunfights and shootouts was our idea of fun as we hid behind cars, around the corner of houses, or porch banisters taking imaginary shots at each other and, occasionally pretending to be dead. Today that scenario with toy guns is likely to get a black child shot by law enforcement officers. Little did we know that our minds were being programmed to view manhood as the ability to dominate by force and, even more so, through a particular lens with white men emerging as the true and dominant male. We participated in our indoctrination, but how could we know that this was merely a different form of Manifest Destiny being programmed subliminally into our minds?

In the early 1970s a more insidious manifestation of this programming occurred, which negatively affected the black community, probably more than any other. Whether intended or unintended by the artists and creators of our mediums of entertainment, movies, television, and music do more to shape our minds than we may know. When *The Godfather* movie came out in 1972, my friends and I adopted aliases with Italian sounding names and began to take on the persona of white characters in the movie. Even though the few references made to the black community in the movie were pejorative, and referred only to white domination of the black community through drug sales, we bought into the hype of *The Godfather*. We adopted the notion of manhood that says the one who kills is a man and the one who can have people killed without getting blood on his own hands is the alpha male. I do not believe *The Godfather* would have influenced the black community in this way if released during the mid-1960s. The prevalence of black male figures like Martin Luther King, Jr., Malcolm X, Mohammed Ali, and a host of new-breed black males in the national spotlight taking a stand for a new image and understanding of manhood had us on a course of community building rather than destruction.

Historically, the hope of the masses of black men was in our ability to fight off those things that seemed to strip us of our ability to be men. The struggle of black manhood versus white manhood was the cause of the disenfranchisement of black voters and property owners during the time of slavery. It may be a little-known fact that free blacks had voting rights in four states at the time of the signing of the Constitution. The black codes and laws were put in place throughout the U.S. to define black manhood as less than, and unequal to, that of white men.

Our hope in this nation always came down to a determination to prove that we were as good as, and equal to white men. This struggle is not limited to men, but I speak of men here because I believe that a redefinition of manhood will redefine womanhood, childhood, national identities and every other paradigm through which we define ourselves in this world. Nevertheless, as black Americans, our hope has always hinged on someone or some group being able to make headway against the opposition to our humanity in order to prove that we were as worthy as any other people to enjoy the benefits of happiness and prosperity in this world. Although it has been almost 150 years since the emancipation of the slaves, we are still trying to prove our equality, and we are still talking about the "first black person" to accomplish something or to hold certain positions as if we are still striving for equality. Perhaps we miss opportunities to express our uniqueness by pressing for equality in every arena. Equal opportunity does not, and perhaps should not, yield equal expression or cookie-cutter outcomes as in the movie *The Truman Show*.

For the first three quarters of the twentieth century, boxing became a vehicle for fighting against the notion that we were inferior to whites. We always felt that, if the odds were even, we could prove that we could hold our own with men of any other race, not only in brute strength but in intelligence and other areas of social progress as well. The insistence of referring to us as animals always reduced us to being defined only by our brute strength, and since this was the arena chosen for us to prove ourselves, we set out to prove that we were stronger, faster, and smarter in that arena. Of course, historically, white men in the North and South set out to prove that that was not the case, so the idea of the "great white hope" was born out of the need to prove their superiority. On the other hand, we always looked for our "great black hope."

In my grandfather's time, in boxing, it was Jack Johnson versus Jim Jeffries. There was no pay per view at that time, but I read accounts of how a nation had their ears to their radios listening to the fight. Blacks were quietly (where it was not safe to show it openly) rooting for Jack Johnson and whites were rooting for Jim Jeffries. The fight took place on July 4, 1910 and billed as the fight of the century. When the fight was over, Jack Johnson was victorious and riots occurred in over twenty-five states and more than fifty cities. My grandfather told my father stories that circulated after that fight. One story he told was that of a black man who went into a restaurant that served whites only and asked for "a cup of coffee as black as Jack Johnson and for two eggs beat up like Jim Jeffries." As the story goes, the white men in the diner jumped up to fight him, and after fighting them all off, with some of them having run out of the diner and some being knocked out on the floor, he leaned over the counter and said to the waiter who was hiding, "I'm still waiting on my eggs."

During my father's time, this scenario repeated itself in the fight between Joe Louis and Max Schmeling, the German fighter. Although the fight promotion publicly symbolized the struggle between U.S. democracy and fascism in Nazi Germany, to many white Americans, Schmeling was their great white hope. In the first fight, Schmeling knocked Louis out in a controversial twelve-round bout, but in the second fight, Louis knocked Schmeling out in the first round on June 22, 1938. During my youth, Mohammed Ali sparked great hope for young black men. Many people viewed the U.S. government's incarceration of Ali and the stripping of his World Heavyweight boxing title as a direct assault on black manhood, in particular, and against black people in general. Ali's defiance with flare made him a hero to us, not only in the U.S. but also in other parts of the world. We stood on street corners and in gyms boxing with rhyme and rhythm echoing Ali's, "I float like a butterfly and I sting like a bee."

In each of these generations, we were trying to find our place in the world as men who could declare themselves men. Unfortunately, each generation of black males to set foot on, or to grow out of, this soil in North America has had to find a definition of manhood that allowed them to survive in a nation and a world that declared them less than men of other races. As we take our place among the peoples of the world, we must find our unique gift that we bring to the world, that unappreciated gift without which the wholeness of our world can never occur. One of the problems I see is that we have tried to become like those who have oppressed and demeaned us. Proverbs 3:31 in the Bible says, "Envy not the oppressor, and choose none of his ways," yet this desire on the part of the oppressed all over the world has helped to maintain oppressive conditions. If a man measures his strength by those around him or even by his enemies, he can only rise to the range of strength that he sees. However, if a man judges his strength by the soul force inside of himself, he will never know his own strength and neither will his enemies. In America, we as black men have measured our strength by the same standards used to oppress us and by those of a society, nation, and world that has defined us as less than and not worthy of being counted as human beings in a world of equals. It is no wonder that we have turned on one another and fallen victim to a definition of ourselves that renders us less than and not equal to other peoples on earth. We have been consistent in our attempts to make ourselves over from the outside, and yet we find ourselves struggling to keep from drowning in the quicksand created by our enemies but maintained and made more deadly by us.

Initially, I distinguish black manhood, from manhood because in this country there has been a concerted effort from the time African slaves were brought here against their will to make sure that black men never reached the status of "men" equal to that of white men. The goal of this book is not to further the battle of the races but to help black men and all people understand how our definition of manhood has been formulated and to help us redefine, not only manhood, but our personhood and our humanity. I believe that we can redefine "manhood" for all men. Perhaps we need a new Declaration of Independence. If it is "self-evident, that all [men] are created equal [and] that they are endowed by their Creator with certain unalienable rights," then we must accept this independence as a gift from God and not from the nation or our foreparents. I believe that, as we do this, we will find less need to blame others and discover the freedom to become new kind of man and a new people. Perhaps our liberation will help others to free themselves from restrictive and limited understandings of manhood and humanity. Perhaps it will successfully challenge those who believe there are inferior and superior races and nationalities of peoples and those who use war to push these beliefs throughout the world.

I want to be clear that I do not believe that the prevailing view of manhood is an American view, even though the American and Western expression of it presently dominates the world. The wielding of power in the world and the means by which the powerful maintain and retain their power is in the blueprint of our worldwide understanding of manhood.

There is no doubt that the world can be a dangerous place, and for some it is very dangerous. The question that I have often asked myself is how can I protect my family from the dangers in the world without becoming like the most dangerous people in the world? How can you protect yourself from violence without having a gun or, in some cases, without being in or protected by a gang, the police, or some military force? I am sure that every child who lives in an area where physical force and group force are the means of control has to ask themselves what they can do to become stronger than those forces or strong enough to protect themselves from those forces. Just saying no to drugs and just saying no to the lure of gang membership has obviously proven to be an ineffective solution to the problems of violence in our inner cities. In a social environment, everyone needs to feel protected, and friends with influence or groups banded together provide that protection. Our law enforcement agencies sworn to protect and serve the community have become a threat themselves to many law-abiding citizens within that community. In some communities, there are multiple threats to safety, and citizens feel vulnerable without a sense of protection at all. I have lived in communities where I felt safer because of the police force protecting the community, and I have lived in communities where I felt as unsafe with the police as I did with the criminal elements in the community. Maybe it was all a matter of perception, but then perception is basic to every social interaction.

The fear and desperation that comes with feeling unsafe and vulnerable leads to many different responses depending on your personality, where you live, how long you have lived there, who you know, and what resources you may have at your disposal to protect you. Young teenagers all over the world raised in violent communities often have very little recourse other than to join a gang. To judge their situation from the outside, even as a close family member, only makes the problem worse. Not only does this further isolate them, but also now, they have no one on the inside or the outside who is able to understand their dilemma. The original intent of gangs was protection and safety for the community. When fighting a corrupt system using the same means used against you only makes you a part of the system you say you are against and, whenever you fight fire with fire, everyone is subject to get burned. Gang prevention is necessary as we see how destructive gang and criminal behavior is to our society, but that only saves a small number of individuals from taking a destructive path. If we talk about and design a plan for gang transformation, we can affect the world and a generation.

When thugs all over the world begin to realize they have modeled themselves after the very system designed to destroy them, we can only hope they will wake up and discover a new model of manhood. The original intent of gangs was to protect the neighborhood not destroy it. It is time for gangs all over the world to protect their neighborhood and protect the weakest people in their neighborhoods rather than preying on them. Those who have been most loyal to their gangs and the thug way of life must go into churches, places of worship, look under every rock, and search the recesses of their own souls to find the God who forgives and restores. Your presence may intimidate some, but do not stop until you have found the Kingdom of God. Do not stop searching until you find one who is willing to tell you why he or she is willing to live with the power of God in the world without fear of death. The Kingdom of God within us is what will transform lives, not religions, churches, or political ideologies. One person with the power of God can bring a nation to its knees. God's power makes the difference, and a forgiven person will not only become powerful but will help others to become powerful as well. When we share the gift of forgiveness, we soon discover that their past failures or successes are never as important as the person is. An army of forgiving and forgiven people is a formidable army. "Let the wicked forsake his way and the unrighteous man his thoughts" (Isaiah 55:7a). "Let him who stole, steal no more" (Ephesian 4:28a). "Let the weak say, I am strong" (Joel 3:10a). Let liars tell the truth, and we will see transformation beyond our wildest imagination.

I too wanted to know about Jesus for whom many people died because of their refusal to deny their allegiance to him. I wanted to study the greatest people of all times to see what I could learn from them to help me to become all that I could become in this world. So I read about some of the great philosophers and some of the great warriors of history. Although I gained many insights from many of the figures in history, the most powerful model of manhood that I have studied, read of, and tried, is the model of Jesus from the Bible. Religion has often painted him as a weak man, but I see him as a very strong and powerful man. When I began to acknowledge God and the reality of His spiritual force in the world, I could not identify with a weak Jesus. The more I learned about him, the more I saw the model of a very different man from the image of him that I had received in the media and in church. I needed a God that was stronger than the forces that I face in the world, attacking me from every direction. I needed a model of manhood that I could follow and not simply worship. The Jesus of much of the Christian church is one to worship and not one to emulate.

It is time for a new understanding of power. We have been operating under the assumption that our greatest strength and power comes from the physical realm. Under our present perception our physical strength, our ability to use life-destroying weapons like guns, knives, bombs, or even our ability to master self-defense and the martial arts are seen as our greatest power and the greatest measure of manhood. Maybe we need to put our spiritual power to the test to see which is greater, the physical power or the spiritual power. The most influential man to ever walk on the earth exercised, taught, and demonstrated spiritual power and his influence is still being felt two thousand years after his physical departure. Encoded in the words and examples he left for us is a formula which, if followed, even thugs and gang members in can play a powerful part in the Kingdom of God that is being established. To acquire this greater power, the masks have to come off.

Chapter Six

Behind the Mask

One of the things we learn from all superhero movies is that behind the mask of the superhero is a person who has seen pain or hurt and has risen to a level of the activation of their internal powers. On the other hand, the villain has had similar experiences of pain and hurt, however, their pain became activated in a negative direction. In a poem Ella Wheeler Wilcox wrote:

> One ship drives east and another drives west
>
> With the selfsame winds that blow.
>
> T'is the set of the sails
>
> And not the gales
>
> Which tells us the way to go.
>
> Like the winds of the seas are the ways of fate,
>
> As we voyage along through life:
>
> T'is the set of the soul
>
> That decides its goal
>
> And not the calm or the strife.

What changes the direction of the soul? What is it if it is not the pain and the hurt? Maybe it is just a sustained hunger to find something truer and greater than we have known. Sometimes as we go back to turning points in our lives, we see signs we missed, and our desire to be a better person helps us change our course to a more positive direction. Every thug and villain was a baby at one time, with some hope of a good future however small. We cannot change the past and the only limit on the future is our grip on the past, not its grip on us.

There are millions of stories worldwide of situations and circumstances that caused lives to take a turn down the road of crime and violence. I talked to a young man whose history is so similar to many young men today. His father died when he was seven years old. His mother could not afford to keep him in a private school where he was doing very well. This once happy child, thrown into an environment governed by fear and violence, became depressed and angry. To escape being bullied he resorted to the language of put downs and verbal cuts that eventually had to be backed up by violence. Mom's work burden and stress of trying to make ends meet, coupled with her own feelings of fear and being unable to cope with life, left her unable to recognize and meet the emotional and safety needs of her son. The turning point for him came when he found acceptance by some of the boys at school. As most boys do, he had to prove himself to be accepted. Perhaps in a different school environment and a different neighborhood his "proving" would not have been so extreme and so far outside the mores of larger society. We do not always have the opportunity to choose our life situations, and sometimes we find ourselves doing what we would not have done in a different time and place.

I spoke to a man in his forties who said that his father was his role model of what not to do. He said his father beat his mother and beat him and his brothers and sister. He saw him drunk a lot. Perhaps headed down the same path as his father, he began selling drugs and wound up in jail. If jail had not served to jar his way of thinking, no doubt he would have become like his father. If we are honest with ourselves, every one of us has had something significant happen to us to change our direction at some point in our lives. Whether by friends, guidance counselors, heroes, or enemies, the lives of others affect our decisions and ultimately our direction in life. It may be easy for us to see that we actually got by with help, and we even give ourselves some slack when it comes to our poor decisions, but often it is difficult to give that same consideration to others. Our understanding of anything affects our judgment of that thing and our understanding of anyone affects how we treat him or her.

Many men fall into negative behavior patterns because they have had no positive male role models. We tend to model what we see. If indeed each of us is the product of what others taught us and modeled for us, then who are we to think that we are better than anyone else simply because we had access to better teaching or modeling? I am not suggesting that we should make excuses for bad or destructive behavior. However, our understanding of behavior, especially our own, will make a world of difference in the way we respond to or attempt to change behavior. If I got out of a bad situation and fail to acknowledge that I got out of it by the grace of God, luck, or the help of others, then my judgment of others in similar situations will close all of those avenues to them. Eventually my blindness to what really helped me will cause me to boast about my own skills, abilities, or intelligence to the extent that I will have convinced myself of my own superiority. It is time to take off our masks and become honest and real.

I had a student who opened up and began to talk to me about his gang involvement and how he was struggling with his life. At one point tears came to his eyes, and he said that his grandmother was the only person he had been able to open up with and share his feelings. I asked him why he and his gang members could not talk about feelings instead of pretending they were too hardcore to have feelings. About six to eight months later his brother killed his grandmother, the only person in his life with whom he could be somewhat honest. Shortly thereafter, both brothers were in the county jail. The country and the world are full of young men who learned to hide their feelings and act tough when being honest with someone might set them free. We have to lose the fear of being vulnerable and do whatever it takes to set ourselves free so that we can also help to free others. If you cannot read, lose the pride and ask a child who reads well to help you learn. Knowledge is power and we must learn as much as we can to make this world a better place for everyone. It is time for the Thug Nation to rise up with new knowledge and new power. It is time for the Thug Nation to meet God. It is time to take off the masks.

I believe when men and women are truly honest before God, the masks will fall off and radical change will take place on all levels of our society. I even believe that gang colors tied together for good and right will have a powerful witness in the world. I have asked gang members, in and out of prison, what it would take to bring unity between gangs, and most of them did not believe it was possible. I believe the answer lies in the face of the thug hidden from public view. The hidden face of most thugs contains a hidden potential for good, and that is the heart when transformed by God that will bring transformation in the world. It is time for a change of heart so that the hidden heart becomes the heart of power. Our greatest power does not come in hiding but in having nothing to hide. Even if you have murdered people in cold blood and hurt many people along the way, there is an opportunity for forgiveness and change. If the God who created us said that we have forgiveness for all of these things, then why would we listen to anyone else? Whether you are a wannabe thug or a wannabe saint, you can change from counterfeit to real by being honest before God and admitting that you have been ignorant and stubborn. When God sees this in us, heaven and earth move on our behalf. This is why he said he did not come into the world to condemn it but to save it. It is not our job to save the world but to be part of the process. We cannot change where we come from, or where anyone comes from, but we can have a new beginning every day and grant others the same privilege. When we realize that fear drives the heart of our enemies, we will seek to destroy the fear in us that will in turn dissolve the fear even in our enemies.

Chapter Seven

A New Conviction

At the core of our present definition of manhood and the systems of power that govern our world is the seed and threat of violence. From parents raising children to nations governing their citizens, force or the threat of force is the ultimate tool for maintaining their power. The system that Jesus introduced to his followers, though seldom practiced, is a system based on freedom from violence but with a power greater than violence. In fact, the Kingdom of Heaven that Jesus talked about is one in which spiritual power is held to be stronger and more powerful than physical power. As thugs and saints all over the world begin to recognize this greater power within, they will be able to see their potential power to transform this world without the use of weapons of violence.

In the Bible, after Jesus wrestled with the decision to avoid death or not as he prayed in the Garden of Gethsemane, a group of Roman soldiers approached him armed to take him by force. When Jesus asked them who they were looking for, they said Jesus of Nazareth, and when he identified himself, the soldiers fell backwards like dead men without a single blow. He even demonstrated power in his conditional surrender, as he only agreed to go with the soldiers if they agreed to let all of his disciples go free. His strength as a man, as far as I can see, is unparalleled, not to mention the fact that he defied death while he lived and conquered it when he died.

No one can know God without a divine encounter. The encounter with God comes with a search, as if you are looking for the greatest treasure in the universe. Being unable to connect with

God is the greatest fear you can have, and once connected, the fear is gone. The Bible says, "There is no fear in love but perfect love destroys fear." When fear is destroyed the only thing that reigns over your life and your world is God. We fight what we fear but if we have no fear, we have nothing to fight. However, wherever love is lacking, fear is inevitable. As I search myself, it seems that either love or fear drives most of my actions. When fear drives my anger, division and separation from others occurs, but when love drives my anger, my righteous indignation allows for restoration and unity. Fear wants to destroy, punish, and banish my enemies and even my potential enemies before they can harm me. When love holds my anger in check, I am always open to re-establish a relationship without needing to destroy, punish, or banish those who have hurt or threatened me. Even my predisposition to do so often relaxes the person who is inclined to harm me. So how can love without fear create an environment where thugs and thieves feel no threat from us and lose their inclination to threaten or harm us? We fear what we do not understand, and in order to understand, we have to ask questions and wait for answers, seek answers, and truly desire to have the answers we seek.

Can a person change their ways and turn from robbing, stealing, and hurting others? I believe the desire do so can be motivated by love without fear displayed by others. While I believe that desire and the willpower to change are essential, I do not believe they are enough to change the mind and heart. I believe only God can do that and I believe that can happen in an event in time or through a series of events. It is the place of divine encounter that all of us must have in order to see our purpose in the big plan. Moses was a murderer before God spoke to him through a burning bush. Our search for God, or to become gods, has led us down many a varied and sundry road as human beings. We have made gods of everything from gold and silver, stone and trees, and even the sun and the stars. Yet our search has left us empty. Even in the strength of their unity, the builders of the Tower of Babel sought to build a structure that would reach into the heavens to find the secrets of the universe but failed, perhaps because they were trying to master the heavens when they had not mastered themselves on earth. Secret societies have claimed to have esoteric knowledge that enables them to unlock deep secrets of life and eternity, but is this for enlightening everyone or for privileging the few?

Stories of the creation of the world are in every culture and the question of where we came from and where we are going seems to be hard-coded in the matrix of every child's mind. While we have answered so many questions over the centuries, we have yet to unlock the door to eternity. Every facet of scientific study is seeking knowledge to answer the myriad of questions that have perplexed us since our inception on this earth. We already enjoy the benefits of scientific discoveries, the benefits of which we use but have no understanding of how or why our technology works. Aside from what the human mind has discovered through our skills of reason, we have what seers and prognosticators call the revealed word or revealed knowledge. Religions, nations, and cultures sprang out of these revelations such as the nation of Israel around which so much of the world is in conflict today.

My intrigue and even my faith go back to a man named Abraham whose faith is foundational in Judaism, Christianity, and Islam. Abraham heard a spiritual voice, believed it to be God, and obeyed it. He left his father's land to follow the directions of a voice he believed to be of a greater God than the god his father worshipped. He set out on a journey to an unknown land directed by the voice of an unseen God. Blessed in his journeying, he learned to trust the voice and protection of his God. He trusted when his God told him he would have a son at 100 years old, and he did. He trusted when the voice told him to sacrifice that son, his only heir, at thirteen years old to a promise from the voice of his God that his offspring would number more than the sand of the sea; and he obediently prepared to do so. Because he believed the voice of his God, millions of people across many nations refer to him as father Abraham today, fulfilling the promise he received from God that through him all of the nations of the earth would be blessed. There is little doubt that his offspring are still here, both natural and spiritual, and that all nations of the earth are the recipients of his faith in God. In fact, we might argue that the effects of his faith and the covenant made with him by the voice of his God figure prominently on the stage of world history and in the current interchange between nations and peoples today. So I ask how did Abraham come to know and hear the voice of God, and can we hear that voice today? The writer of the book of Hebrews says that those who will come to God must first believe that God exists and that those who seek him most determinedly will find the presence of God. Another writer describes God as the creator of all things, the giver of life, in whom we live, move, and have our very being, who we can know intimately if we search diligently.

    I am calling all thugs to take the risk of pursuing this God, not joining a church or a religion but something so much greater, the Kingdom of Heaven. You do not have to be a member of a church or religion to be a soldier in the army of the God. Jesus said, "I came that you might have abundant life, just not selfishly" (John 10:10). It is time to share the wealth and live more than just for ourselves. If anyone has lack, we all have lack, and we should not be satisfied until every broken heart is healed and every prisoner set free. It is time for thugs to talk to each other and to God. It is time to pull back the curtain and reveal the wizard so that those who have hoarded the wealth of this world can begin to share, but it must begin with us. It is time to pledge allegiance to the highest God with the same blood-in-blood-out dedication that you have followed, not abandoning your heart for your fellow gang members or boardroom members, but with a greater heart for them.

Many headed down the road to becoming thugs and many who were thugs, changed because of conversations among friends. Friends talking about life and their hopes for the future can often change their life direction. In high school, four friends and I decided we would go to college together, become successful, make a lot of money, and do great things to change our world. As one of those friends recently chided me about, I remained in Cleveland when the others went because I fell in love. One became the president of a university, another who recently passed away became successful in finance, one died early, and I lost track of the fourth friend. Here again, conversation can bring inspiration and motivation. Thinking back on my own experience reminds me of the four young men out of Newark, New Jersey, who talked among themselves and made a pact to go to college and become doctors. They persevered and, after becoming successful, they wrote a bestseller entitled *The Pact*.

Inspired by talking to my friends as we hung out together, I remember talking about how good it would be if there were playgrounds and areas in the community to just go and talk. It seemed, however, that every time we congregated as young black men we were perceived as gathering to do harm rather than something positive. However, our talks inspired me and taught me how emotional release and the cultivation of creative imagination can come through conversation. Maybe we need more directed conversations to include more than one generation, such as often takes place in barbershops in the black community. Maybe such conversations would inspire and motivate more thugs, and would-be thugs, to find solutions to community problems. Neighbors used to talk to each other over the clothesline, over their gardens, or just sitting on the steps of their homes or apartments. Thugs on the stoop, it is time to start having some real talk about how, through your organization, you can become positive change agents for a world on the brink of destruction. It is time for all of us, on all levels, to come out of isolation and begin to see that we need each other and that, by working together, nothing will be impossible for us. Our conversations must be more than about money and our personal success.

With all of our knowledge of human behavior and with all of the social progress we have made throughout the world, the blight in the poorest communities is getting worse. We looked for solutions in social programs or political gestures, but the problem continues to grow as evidenced by the expansion of the Thug Nation. We have looked for solutions through religion and religious institutions, but in areas where gangs and gang violence are prevalent, the religious institutions are under siege and without power. I am convinced that the answer is in the transformation of the mind, the heart, and the soul. Although it has become such a cliché, Jesus' words about being born again, if reexamined by thugs, may prove to be more powerful than what many churches and religious people have discovered in the last two centuries.

Throughout history, God opens secrets and revelations little by little that further the plan of bringing the Kingdom of Heaven to earth. Often these revelations have come through the most despised and rejected people of the world and in communities where people are the most heavily burdened. I believe the time is ripe for us to see the fulfillment of the words of the prophet Jeremiah. If my senses are correct, God is preparing people all over the world in surprising ways and through the least expected people. In the book of Jeremiah chapter 31:33 the prophet says that God showed him that he would establish a new covenant in the earth in which he would put his law within our hearts and in our minds. He went on to say that no one would have to tell another person to know God because they would all know him from the least to the greatest because God would forgive them for everything they have done and remember their sins no more. An external law does not govern the person that lives by an internal divine law (Galatians 5:22-23).

Imagine an army of former thugs on every level operating with a new mind and spirit, proving that the spiritual power is greater than weapons of violence. It is an army of self-ruled soldiers governed by the voice of God in their hearts. The book of Proverbs says, "He that has no rule over his own spirit is like a city that is broken down and without walls" (25:28). As we take control of our own spirits, we rebuild cities of power. When an army of self-ruled soldiers came together in an upper room, waiting to hear from God, an amazing thing happened as recorded in the biblical book of Acts chapter 2. Who knows what God will do with such an army today? I say let us put it to the test to see if spiritual power has the power to transform this world today. I am not suggesting that this will be easy and that a number of thugs will not have to die at the hands of each other and law enforcement officers in order to make this happen, but for the sake of humanity, it is worth the try.

Those convicted by the education system as unable to read, write, or learn must establish a new conviction and determine to make knowledge their aim, learning from anyone who is willing to share knowledge. Reading is essential because it is the key to certain kinds of knowledge that are necessary for self-rule. Those convicted of crimes who are sitting in prisons around the world must have a personal conviction to read, study, and engage in conversations within prisons to break down the barriers that have divided soldiers who should be in the same army. Those who run the streets from behind prison bars must send out a new message that every foot soldier must learn to read and write. The message must be emphatic that they must learn about the laws, which work for and against their communities, and ask God for wisdom in how to free their communities from the train that sends young men and women from school, to the streets, to prison or the grave. I know this is a life risking proposition for gang leaders all over the world, but if you have made it this far defying death, why not take the risk of dying for something as powerfully world changing as joining an army of God?

While teaching at the alternative school, known in the community as the prison school, I decided that if I was serious about changing the lives of young men and women headed to prison or an early grave, I had to be fearless and willing to sacrifice my own life. When threatened by students, I sometimes would just look at them and ask, "How are you going to kill a dead man?" I had quoted Romans 12:1-2 many times, but now I had the opportunity to make my body a living sacrifice and test my theory that spiritual power is the greatest power. My first day in the high school classroom one student looked me up and down and asked, "How long are you going to be here?" I told him that I was the permanent teacher and he responded, "You wait until Slick gets back," (referring to a student who had been suspended). "We're going to run you up out of here." I looked at him calmly and said, "I welcome the challenge." He missed a few days of school and I called his home and asked mother about his absence. He returned to school the next day, walked down the hallway to my classroom door, pointed his finger in my face and said, "Don't ever call my house again." He then turned around and walked out of the school. He missed a few more days, and again I called his home and spoke to his mother. His mother told me that she was hoping that he would go ahead and finish high school and that she would appreciate my help. He came to school the next day pointed his finger in my face again and said, "Maybe you didn't hear me. I told you don't ever call my house again." The student whom I will refer to as Smooth-G, turned to walk out of the school again when I asked, "Do you remember what you told me my first day in this class? You told me that you were going to run me out of here." I paused a moment and said, "You've got to be here in order to run me out." From the look on his face, I could tell my words gave him pause but he left school that day anyway. A day or so later the school secretary, who had heard about the exchange between Smooth-G and me, told me that she had his father's telephone number and wanted to know if I would like to call him. I called his father and met him on a Saturday morning where we talked for a couple of hours. His father, recently released from the federal penitentiary, informed me that he had not been in his son's life very much; he was in prison for most of his son's upbringing. He told me that his son was trying to follow his footsteps as a kingpin drug dealer and that he was doing all he could to show his son that he did not want that life. He asked me to do whatever I could to help his son graduate from high school and take a different track, and I told him I would do my best.

Smooth-G came to school the following Monday with the same tough act, still threatening me because I called his father, but this time he stayed in school. I checked with the school guidance counselor to see how many credits he needed to graduate, and it turned out that he could graduate within one year, at the age of nineteen, if he worked hard enough. There were still days that he would walk out of class and miss days of school to handle his drug business, but for the most part he would come to school and work. Once or twice, he was out of school because he was in the county jail. Perhaps probation and an ankle bracelet so the court system could track his whereabouts helped him to stay in school. When in school he challenged me every day, and often would do outlandish things just to see if he could throw me off balance. He would tell me that I could not teach him anything if I was not teaching him how to make more money, and he made constant attempts to disrupt the class.

One day he blurted out in class, "Mr. Tucker, you're a preacher aren't you?" I said yes. He then said, "The Bible says turn the other cheek doesn't it?" Again, I said yes. He responded, "what would you do if I just walked up to you and slapped you across your face (as he slapped his hand demonstrating how he would smack me). Would you turn the other cheek?" I said, "Well, Smooth-G, I may turn the other cheek, and I may not turn the other cheek, but you know what? I don't want to find out what I would do, and I don't think you want to find out what I would do since our relationship seems to be working the way it is. Why don't we just leave it that way?" He laughed and the class laughed, so no respect was lost on either side. Teachers began to talk about how much he respected me, and one relative who worked in the school told me that, at family gatherings, Smooth often talked respectfully about me. In the end, with the help of an outstanding job coach, a dedicated school principal, and concerned teachers and staff, Smooth-G graduated from high school. It really does take a village to raise a child, and without a concerted effort on all of our parts to save our children of every age, we are going to lose the village.

Many of our black youth may need special education intervention and specialized assistance simply because of their environment, I am convinced that their immediate needs are more physical, social, remedial, and motivational than cognitive in nature. One child I worked with in the therapeutic setting, diagnosed as ADHD (Attention Deficit Hyperactivity Disorder) and BD (Behavior Disorder), responded to an unconventional method of modifying his behavior. I worked with him when he was in seventh grade. His mother stopped giving him medication, and each afternoon he became very agitated, hyperactive, and out of control to the point of requiring physical restraint. I perceived that he was a very bright kid because of his social skills with other students and his acumen for manipulation. One day I asked him to step out of the classroom because he was putting demands on the teacher and disrupting the class. I told him that if he could stand completely and utterly still for two minutes without moving his head or any muscle in his body I would grant the request he had made of the teacher. He agreed and I took out my cell phone, opened the digital timer, and began the challenge. At first he lasted about three seconds, but because he wanted to prove that he could do it and because he really wanted the privilege he had demanded, I allowed him to try again and again until he was able to stand completely still for two minutes. As he was able to succeed and gain the privilege he desired, his sense of pride in himself was evident. I used the method with him until I left that setting. Eventually he was able to control himself and stand still for periods of five minutes at a time. Whenever he did this exercise, his behavior was under control for two to three hours, and on those days no physical restraint was necessary and his behavior problems were minimal.

Unfortunately, I saw this student a few years later at the alternative high school where he went after his introduction to the streets and gang initiation put him on house and school arrest. In addition to the previous labels, he had the new label of bipolar disorder. I told him that he had been diagnosed as ADHD, BD, learning disabled, and bipolar because someone did not understand how his energy and mind worked. I told him that I had shown him the tools he needed to understand, gain control of, and manage his own energy.

When I worked with high school and middle school students, I used this exercise with many other students as well. Once, I did this exercise with eleven students at once who were able to stand perfectly still for ten minutes. The pride and change in their behavior that day was greater than with previous students. In each case, it seemed to surprise the students themselves that they could have that much self-control. One thing that has been essential for this or any method I use is my knowledge of the student. I have found that the more I know about a student, the more effectively I can teach him or her. I make a point of interviewing each student I work with so that I can understand their background, family history, learning style, interests, and areas where they have a personal sense of accomplishment or failure in their lives. I also interview and observe them so that I can understand their temperaments, i.e., what made them anxious, angry, excited, agitated, and enthusiastic.

Special Education pedagogy and methodology support the idea that one size does not fit all and that an individualized plan needs to be in place for each student. Special Education training and practices do not seem to do as well taking into consideration the cultural, social, and ethnic exigencies out of which each student has been nurtured. Whether by design or as an unintended by-product, young black males are overrepresented in special education, the prison system, and the graveyard. I believe there is a direct correlation between all three, not to mention domestic violence, unemployment, drug abuse, and mental health disorders.

In the educational settings I have worked in, as well as other settings such as prison ministry, youth mentoring, and rites-of-passage youth programs, most of the boys and girls I worked with did not have their fathers in their lives in any significant way. This is where thugs can step up to the plate and have a positive impact on their own children and the community. Once while working with eight to ten male students in my classroom I encouraged them to come to terms with their anger and hurt from not having their fathers in their lives as a positive, powerful, and loving role model. Because of my personal knowledge of each student and the similarities of each of their stories, I felt safe in going around the room, with their permission, identifying the things each of them could forgive their fathers for, and showing them they were following the same path. I talked to them about ways to achieve a level of manhood that would allow them to understand their fathers, the world their fathers were up against, and how to be different from their fathers. As I went around the room, I told one student, "You are angry with your father because he has been in prison for eight years and he is so far away that you only get to see him once a year, if that." I told another student, who was eighteen years old at the time, "Your life turned sour when your father was killed when you were eleven years old." To another student I said, "You are so angry with your father for beating your mother, you, your brothers and sisters, and then abandoning you that you don't know how to be a man or how to treat a woman." As I went around the room I saw tears well up in some eyes and anger in others, but there was no doubt that I was bringing true and hidden emotions to the surface.

Until we honestly address the myriad of familial, social, and emotional issues with and for these students, they will continue to fill the prisons and the morgues. This not only affects black youth, but also the larger society and the world. Many school systems have gang prevention programs, but seldom do we question whether gangs have functional roles in communities, which could produce a positive rather than negative outcome. Lack of enthusiasm and lack of motivation logically lead to identification for special education, which leads to their delinquency. All of my students in the alternative high school setting were in special education and were in gangs or seriously affected by them. The students I visited in the county jail were there because of their connections to gangs. However, most of them were able to think on a higher level when it came to adaptation to the streets but were deficient academically yet not cognitively. Now that I am working in an elementary school setting, I have found that the methods I mentioned above continue to prove effective, and I discover new methods as I learn from them each day. Perhaps there are no static methods of teaching that work for every student and in every setting, but perhaps, our methodologies should be wells to draw wisdom from as we adapt to every situation.

The bottom line in some situations is that students respond better when they know you care about them as a person and that you are going to be honest with them. Many of the young men and women I worked with had shot and robbed people. Some even wore their gunshot wounds as badges of honor. I visited one student who was up on charges for murder in the county jail. Most of the young men and women I worked with were angry, and listening to their life stories, I understood why. One year before going from the therapeutic setting to the alternative school setting, I asked the principal if I could come to the high school to talk to some of the young men. I wanted to get a better understanding of how and if I could help them become successful. The principal pulled a group of fifteen boys from the gymnasium who were playing basketball and brought them to a classroom for our discussion.

As the boys entered the room, they first complained about having their basketball time cut short. I observed them as they derided each other about the way they played basketball or the clothes they wore. I started by asking them what they wanted to do with their lives after they finished school. Some of them kept bantering back and forth, so I had to shift my focus to theirs in order to bring their attention to a different focal point. I told them that their success depended upon how well they applied what they were naturally good at to everything they did in life. One of the comedians turned his comedy towards me, so I replied, "You would make a good comedian, but you have to know that it is going to take a lot of work because right now all I hear is your ability to crack on other people." After the class laughed, I had a chance to address the personalities of a few other students. I told one young man, "You are a thinker; you like to know what's going on before you jump into something." To another one I said, "You are a follower. You just go along with the strongest voice." With each character read I did, the class confirmed that my assessment was true from what they knew about their classmates and others asked me what I saw in them.

Having gained their attendance and a modicum of their respect, I said, "I am here to talk to you about your power and how to use it." Of course, they all had to brag at that point about their power.

I asked them where their power came from, and most of them began to talk about guns. Since they were determined to talk about guns I said, "Almost all of you are in this school because of your tempers. Your temper is like a gun and it can do a lot of damage. I am not here to take your gun away from you." At that point, I had their undivided attention. One student, being somewhat facetious, said, "You mean I can keep my gun?" I said, "Yes, I am not here to take your gun away from you. I'm here to teach you how to use it. I want you to have your gun. You are going to need it for life, but a gun in the hands of someone who does not know how to use it is likely to shoot themselves, babies, even their own mother. You see your temper is like a gun, and if you do not know how to use it, you will hurt someone, mostly those who are close to you and yourself." Since that time, I have been on a mission to help young people manage what I call the fire in their bellies, their anger.

Chapter Eight

Self-Rule

Someone once said, "You can't teach what you don't know, and you can't lead where you won't go." I soon realized that I had to demonstrate everything I was trying to teach, and that my credibility with the young men and women I was working with was not dependent on what I told them, but on what I showed them with my own life. The Bible says in Proverbs 25:28, "He that has no rule over his over spirit is like a city that is broken down and without walls." On the flip side, to rule your spirit is like ruling a city, and a fortified city is a place of great commerce and peace. Therefore, I challenge my students, and anyone who will listen, to discipline themselves in every way possible because the greatest power available to us is inside of us. Our desire for food, sex, money, things, power over others, and so many other things rule the lives of all of us at some point, but to have control over ourselves in each of these areas will bring out our greatest potential.

One of my students who always had money in his pocket and always dressed impeccably told me that I could not teach him anything if I was not teaching him how to make more money. He would sit in class and talk about how much money he made selling drugs. He would often miss school at the beginning of each month because he had to make his rounds because that is when his customers received their government checks. Once he said to me that I should come and work for him because he could pay me more than the school system. When I responded that money did not rule me, and that his money did not impress me, he tested me for weeks to see if he could find flaws in my reasoning based on what I said. I turned social studies lessons and civics lessons into opportunities to teach them about how government works and who benefits most. I taught them that money was a tool of exchange but that it was not the only tool or the only way to have more in life. We talked about how money can work for or against them. We talked about forms of government and examined the form of government used in gangs and military organizations. Then we talked about how the power of knowledge and self-rule as a source of wealth and power can be greater than the power of money. They were not always convinced, but I am sure that our lively discussions planted seeds for them to think about.

As we continued our conversation involving the job coach and other teachers and staff from the school, we brainstormed ways we could take some of the power out of money through alternative methods of acquiring wealth or the things we want. Perhaps with a mission and a method, thugs could build their own legal empires. Emphasizing that knowledge gives them power, I told them about the skills that my mother and father taught me coming up. I said that for years I did my own auto repair, plumbing, electrical, masonry, and woodwork to take care of the homes I lived in. I told them of a $3,500 estimate I had for car repair, which I did for myself for less than $150 by purchasing the parts and doing the work myself. I told them that money saved is money earned. I also told them of the sewing, cooking, and gardening skills I learned from my parents and how I had used all of those skills to save money and live better.

I encouraged them to think about self-rule as the highest form of government. I encouraged them to think about how self-management can lead to greater and greater degrees of self-sufficiency. I suggested that they find relatives or community members who have a skill and ask them to teach it to them. I suggested that they learn basic skills about many things from YouTube or the internet. While the discussion intrigued them, they all suggested that it was just easier to have money in order to be happy. When I saw their enthusiasm and intrigue with our discussion topics, I realized that even thugs are inspired when they catch a vision of becoming part of positive change for themselves and their community.

In order for change to take place in a community, or on a society-wide basis, it must first take place in individuals who can think independently enough to bring positive influence to the world around them. Without the ability to rule ourselves, no plan for social change will be effective. To bring out the spiritual power that is available to us we have to master our appetites. We must master our appetites for sex, money, and power. Any appetite we do not master is an open door for personal failure with community-wide consequences as well. None of us is exempt from temptation, but our failures and our successes over temptation produce our strength, and both can help strengthen our communities and those around us. For all of us sex, money, and power play a significant role in our lives, but we must ask ourselves whether our use of them benefits or hurts others. The account of Jesus' temptation by Satan after forty days in an isolated place without food provides a model for us of the power of self-rule.

Our greatest power in this world is not in ruling over others or material things but in ruling over ourselves. I learned as a teenager that what I feared most would control me for the rest of my life. As I have recognized my fears over the years, I have wrestled within myself to overcome them. It was my fear of fear that helped me to push through some difficult places. Driven by a fear of fear, many of us would not do things we did if we were not afraid of what others thought of us. This is the fear that drives people into gangs, clicks or exclusive groups. True self-management is being able to manage fear and honestly face fears when they arise. Fear is often associated with shame, but I have found that my greatest shame comes when I am not honest about my fears or when I cannot admit them and face them.

Having run from bullies in my early teens, my greatest freedom came when I faced my fears and my bullies. Victory over my fears and my bullies taught me one of my most valuable life lessons; the only way to overcome my fears is to face them. It was such a valuable lesson and feeling of liberation for me that I reiterated to my son over and over as he was growing up in urban New Jersey that, no matter who or what he had to face, I wanted him to make up his mind that he would never be afraid of anyone. I knew the streets were tough and that he would face the challenge of gangs and bullies, and I knew that I could not fight his battles for him. As a parent, it was difficult to let him face some things alone, but I told him that it was better to die unafraid, or at least being determined not to allow fear to rule him, than it would be to live his life in perpetual fear. While I believe this was a valuable lesson for him, I wish I had been able to teach him more about how to overcome the greater fears of failure, success, and hard work.

I often wondered why the people who topped the list of folks going to hell in the book of Revelations were the fearful and unbelieving. I asked why not murderers or adulterers? I discovered that fear is the thing that blocks everything progressive or good in life. Fear prevents you from taking a risk to learn something different or do something different. Fear can prevent you from doing the good that you know to do, which is tantamount to doing evil. It is almost as if fear itself is looking for a mind, heart, or body to inhabit and it slips in through every crack or crevice it can find. Every time I overcame a fear, my world opened up with new possibilities, but the more fears I faced, the more my world opened to show me that I would always have new fears to face. I thought when I faced the fear of death that I had conquered my greatest fear. However, I have come to realize that anyone can have a death wish, and that a willingness to die, even a desire to die, can reveal fears that are greater than the fear of death. Fear of failure can be greater than the fear of death. Fear of success can be greater than the fear of death. Even fear of being responsible for ourselves can be greater than the fear of failure, success, or death. Yet, for as long as I can remember, I have had a vision of success inside and the belief that I have something significant to contribute to the world. My challenge has been finding out how to release it. One day I realized that the release valve is inside, not outside. Nothing outside of me could destroy me unless I let it get inside of me. I did not realize this until I was at a very low place in my life. It was only when I ran out of options that I could see my way. I call this the discipline of disappointment because disappointment and dissatisfaction have pushed me into new places that ultimately blessed me.

One day, when I was very depressed about how my life was going, having gained so much weight, and having lost sight of my dreams and visions, I lay in bed emotionally paralyzed. I discovered that if I did not muster every bit of strength within me, I would die without ever doing what I believed I was on earth to accomplish. At that point, I realized that I had to draw strength from every fiber of my being that would respond to me. Unable to force myself out of bed, a strategy came to mind that might work. I made an agreement with myself that my word to myself would be my bond. Whatever I told myself to do, I would do it, and I would not break my word to myself. I guess because my father was a man of his word, and I valued that, it had become important for me to be a man of my word. Unfortunately, I had given my word in places that I had not kept. Now I realized that my life depended not on my keeping my word to someone else but to myself. I would only tell myself to do what I knew I could do, and then I would set conditions for myself that would help me to do it.

That morning lying in bed trying to get up to run and get some exercise in, I decided I would take baby steps and bite-size pieces. I said to myself, "On the count of three, you are going to put one foot out from under the cover." Although it may not sound like much of an accomplishment, to someone who is depressed, this could be a major feat. I counted again to put my leg out from under the covers, and then my other foot, and so on, until I was able to get out of bed. I began to use this method in my exercise routine. I would tell myself that I was going to run ten steps, and then down the driveway and back, and so on. As days, weeks, months, and years went by using this strategy and keeping my word to myself, eventually I was able to run miles and miles a day, sometimes topping fifty miles a week, running competitively, and training and motivating others to run as well. This strategy also became a tool to help me face other fears and challenges in my life. As I gained rule over my own spirit, my whole life changed.

Using this strategy for reading, writing, or learning anything difficult enabled me to see that I could accomplish anything I set my mind to achieve. When I saw the power of keeping my word to myself, I began to challenge myself to do things that felt emotionally impossible, but which I knew I was fully capable of doing. The power of my word and doing exactly what I said I would helped me understand why God had to confound the language of those who tried to build the tower of Babel. When words and deeds line up together, anything is possible. If I did not want to discipline myself to do something, or if I did not feel strong enough to keep my commitment to myself, I would not give myself my word until I knew I would keep it. Sometimes I had to say it aloud to someone else to reinforce my determination to keep my own word.

In order to regain our balance in this world I believe we need to restore the power of our word. Broken promises and broken words have landed us in a place where we cannot even trust ourselves. We must restore balance within before we can restore balance to the world around us. We must manage ourselves in order to manage our world. My word must hold value to me before it can hold value to you. While this may seem to be insignificant, all power and power relationships require consistency of delivery. This consistency of delivery is what makes the world go round and keeps us in balance. As long as the sun consistently delivers its energy to the earth, we can survive and thrive, but if it became a supernova or a black hole, it would disrupt all life on earth. Even the founders of governments realize the power of contract that comes with giving our word. At one time, a handshake or simply the giving of one's word was sufficient to establish a binding contract, but broken words and inconsistent delivery of promises made it necessary for written contracts and physical means of enforcement.

As our word becomes more powerful, we will rebuild places in our world where hope has been lost. As our communication becomes clearer and more effective, we will rebuild communities, redirecting our energy from litigating and fighting each other to helping one another. When I pray, "Thy Kingdom come, on earth as it is in heaven," this is the vision of what I see coming to earth. This vision does not require more sophisticated and strategic political maneuvering or more law enforcement. Rather it requires a growing and contagious determination to rule ourselves. If we rule ourselves from the inside, there is no need for rule from the outside. I have found that ruling my appetites has given me power over my need for external constraints. Mustering the discipline to exercise and control my desire for certain foods, has enabled me to avoid medicines and enjoy my life in this body in ways I could not before. While much of this I was able to do by sheer willpower, I found out that my willpower alone was not strong enough. When I called on God, I received help in my spirit that was greater than any power I could muster on my own. Sometimes this help came through another person, and sometimes it seemed to come from an open window to heaven. As I began to exercise my spiritual, physical, mental, and emotional muscles, I experienced a greater degree of power in my life. The greater revelation for me was the realization of the collective potential we have if we individually rule our own spirits and reconnect with God.

Years ago, I read a book on spiritual leadership in which there was a chapter entitled, "Send Every Man a Leader." If we are all leaders, we can only be leaders of ourselves and not of other people. As we lead ourselves, we learn from and share with others, which will ultimately strengthen us individually and collectively. When I think of God's kingdom coming on earth, as it is in heaven, I think of people who are ruled by internal rather than external laws. I think of the word that came to the prophet Jeremiah in which God said, "After those days, says the Lord, I will put my law in their inward parts, and write it in their hearts; and will be their God, and they shall be my people. And they shall teach no more every man his neighbor, and every man his brother, saying, Know the Lord: for they shall all know me, from the least of them unto the greatest of them, says the Lord: for I will forgive their iniquity, and I will remember their sin no more" (Jeremiah 33:33b-34). This is the vision of the Kingdom of Heaven that looms large in my spirit. It is a return to the Garden of Eden where there was no need for external laws because the internal law is the ruling force. It is an invitation to have God as leader, captain, and governor of our lives, not as an external force over us but as an internal power within us. It is an opportunity to do what the people of Israel rejected when God invited them to come to the foot of the mountain to experience divine glory and communication with God. Through this vision, I see God saying to thugs and saints, "Call on me and I will answer you, and show you great and mighty things" (Jeremiah 33:3).

When we call on God, we have to "come correct" as they say in one common vernacular. Coming correct to God involves some kind of sacrifice of will and temperament in order to come into the presence of God, mentally, physically, spiritually, and emotionally. Just as electrical power needs a conduit that can handle the current that flows through it, spiritual power needs a sufficient vehicle to flow through as well. Many people like the idea of being able to experience the presence of God with all of its benefits, but very few people seem to be willing to go through the discipline that is required to live there. Just as certain levels of electrical voltage cannot flow through thin or weak wires, certain levels of spiritual power cannot flow through certain states of human behavior or mentality. For example, an overly egotistical person cannot open the door of their heart, mind, or spirit to allow even the thought of another person's ideas or the input from a divine source. When we are self-consumed, our world is all about us.

Astronomers estimate that there are over 400 billion stars in our galaxy alone and that our sun is not even one of the largest stars in our galaxy. It is estimated that there are over 100 billion galaxies in the universe with over a septillion stars (that is the number one with twenty-four zeros after it). Given the vastness of our universe, it is amazing that our egos can allow us to think that we are the most important planet in the universe. Individually we often act as though what is important to us is the most important thing on earth. In the story of Adam and Eve, and in many mythological accounts of how we as human beings fell from grace or failed to reach grace, our desire to be the most important or most powerful led to our downfall. There are spiritual laws seared in our conscience, which when obeyed, allow us to release our greatest spiritual power. Once again, God said, "I will place my laws in their minds and write it on the table of their hearts" (Jeremiah 31:33). We have to become masters of ourselves in order to discover what God has placed inside of us. We have to spend time with God in order to hear from heaven, and we have to ask for wisdom and uncommon sense to discipline our appetites so that the light of God can shine powerfully in us. It is not our appetites that will destroy us but our inability to control them. Just as our appetites are the portals to our minds and emotions, our thoughts become the gatekeepers, which direct them. It has been important for me to remember, however, that I am not my mind or my thoughts but that I have the power to control my mind and my thoughts with help from God and godly sources.

One day, with students listening in on a lively exchange between six or seven male co-workers in my high school classroom, the question of religion entered the discussion. One man insisted that religion was the cause of so much division in the world, and he expressed his disdain for religion and religious leaders. As he knew I was a minister, he expected me to come to the defense of Christianity. However, to his surprise, I agreed with him. I wrote the names of the major religions on the board, and I drew an arrow pointing upward above each religion. I explained to him that each religion pointed to a God or reality above itself that represented the creator of everything that exists or the most powerful being or essence in the universe. I suggested that if each of those religions continued to look beyond itself, to pursue God, it would never be able to put itself up as a religion superior to another religion. I then suggested that the problem of religion occurs when the religion itself becomes a God. That is to say that when the religion points to itself, it becomes ineffective in pointing to God. I expressed my belief that, while religions may hold sacred texts with valuable knowledge about God and all of creation, religions often become the barrier to our search for God and our desire for godliness. All of a sudden, we seemed to be on the same page, and our conversation could focus on the good things that need doing rather than on the religion that was or was not doing those things.

While I do not subscribe to the belief that religion is going to be our salvation on earth, I wholeheartedly believe that we will not survive on this planet without recognizing and acknowledging God. I have drawn nuggets of truth and valuable knowledge from religious sources other than Christianity, and I never want to be so arrogant as to suggest that I know the way better than anyone else or that my religious or spiritual practices are superior to anyone else's. I am not so naïve to believe that Christianity has or will be our salvation. In fact, I am fully aware that Christianity was a strong tool of colonization, slavery, apartheid, Jim Crow, and many other crimes against humanity. I had almost rejected the Bible and Christianity as the white man's religion until I read a book by a Hindu Swami entitled *The Sermon on the Mount* in which he described Jesus' sermon as the most powerful message ever delivered. As I began to read the words of Jesus and examine the account of his life, I was intrigued to the point of wondering why Christianity, as I had experienced it, did not portray Jesus in this more powerful light.

Reading the words of Jesus and examining his stated purpose for coming to earth almost seems to oppose the message of Christianity in many respects. I believe that Jesus would receive the same response from religious and political leaders today that he received in his day. I remember hearing a story of a black man who went into a white church in the South during the days of Jim Crow. Turned away because of his skin color, he met Jesus passing by as he walked away from the church. Jesus asked him why he was so sad and downcast in spirit, and he explained that he tried going into the church but they would not let him in. Jesus responded, "Don't feel bad, my friend. I have been trying to get into that church for years and they won't let me in either." Just as churches rejected people based on their race or skin color, I am afraid that they continue to turn people away from God in so many other ways that we trivialize. This is not only true of Christianity but of any religion, religious organization, or teaching which points to itself as the ultimate authority rather than God. Regardless of which religious belief we say we live by, the code of our hearts reflected in our actions reveal our true beliefs. As governors and rulers of our own hearts, we manage the most powerful system of government, corporation, or network on earth. If we manage ourselves well, the world will change and God will help us.

The great King Solomon prayed to God for help for present and future generations. He asked God to forgive anyone who would ask for forgiveness, acknowledge God, recognize their faults, and manage their lives better. God's response to his prayer was:

> *If my people, which are called by my name, shall humble themselves, and pray, and seek my face, and turn from their wicked ways; then will I hear from heaven, and will forgive their sin, and will heal their land. (2 Chronicles 7:14)*

The ball is in our court. We simply have to govern ourselves, rule our thoughts, and discipline our spirits. God is the King of the Universe, and each one of us holds the office of prince or princess of our own spirits. Serving well in this office increases our power as individuals, and our influence grows because we reflect to others what they can become when they too are able to rule themselves well and submit to the King of the Universe. In so doing, we become a mighty army of God for the Kingdom of Heaven on earth.

Chapter Nine

Calling Moms and Dads

Yes, I believe God is calling forth an army of sincere people who believe that God is the Master of the universe, and yes, I believe thugs will play a great role in the restoration of earth to the Kingdom of God. However, I believe that moms and dads of all ages can and must play a significant role in this process.

This is not a time to look back at all of the wrong things done by any of us. This is a time to seize the moment of forgiveness and become part of the greatest army ever. Where we destroyed, we will build. Where we hurt, we will heal. Where mother's hearts have been broken for their children, they will mend. A generation of children taught to move with the heartbeat of God is rising to change the way we teach and learn. What role can a mother play if she is fearful of her son either leaning towards or being threatened by the thug life? What role can fathers play? What role can men play who have not been involved in their children's lives?

I have found that living with regrets will kill time and detract from my forward progress. We have all done things we wish we had not done and made choices we wish we had not made, but harboring regrets is not a productive use of time. Although we cannot turn back the hands of time, and we cannot do a day over until we get it right like the main character in the movie *Ground Hog Day*, we can use our memories to create positive change. Just as scientific progress builds on knowledge gained from successful and failed experiments, we can use the knowledge and wisdom we gain from our mistakes, tragedies, misfortunes, and our successes to build a better future.

I want to speak first to the mothers. It has been said that the "hand that rocks the cradle, rules the world." If that kind of power lies in the hands of mothers, then I believe the mothers of thugs, the mothers of would-be thugs, and the mothers of those threatened and intimidated by thugs can play a significant role in our progress to save the human family and spread the influence of the Kingdom of Heaven on earth. I don't know the pain a mother feels when she sees her son threatened by the violence that is so prevalent in many of our schools and on many of our streets, but I have to tell you, mothers, that you, perhaps more than anyone else, are in a position to change the violence and bring health to our communities. You are the ones who enroll them in schools, tell them how long to stay outside to play, take them or not take them to church, decide which entertainment you will pay for and where they can play, and you show them the disposition and attitude they must take towards life. The things you are angry about and the things that are important to you are going provide direction for your sons and your daughters.

As mothers, you have sacrificed for your children, but we need a new kind of sacrifice from you. We need mothers who will sacrifice their sons as Hannah did Samuel in the Bible when she turned him over to the Lord, trusted God to take care of him. Mothers, I know this is a tremendous sacrifice because a mother's instinct is to protect her children from danger. To sacrifice your children to the streets and to an environment of bullying in our schools, trusting God to take care of them, is a going to take a lot of faith. You cannot protect them on the playground, in the restroom at school, or on the way to and from school. I know you fear for your child's safety, but your fear can handicap your child and put them in greater danger. Mom, if you can sacrifice some of your healthy and unhealthy fear, which makes you protective and more often over-protective, then you will have an opportunity to see God work in amazing ways. You have sacrificed for your children out of love and out of fear, but now we need you to sacrifice your fear on the altar of love.

When you fear for your son's safety, you automatically want to protect him and fight for him. Some battles you must fight for your children; however, some battles they must fight for themselves. If not allowed to fight their own battles, win or lose, fear will be the driving force in their lives. Some battles you can fight side by side with your sons or daughters showing them how to face their fears without giving in to the pressures of breaking the law or doing wrong. If you are a praying mom, your prayers and beliefs will mean more to your sons and daughters when you demonstrate them confidently under adverse conditions. When they see how the power of your faith moves the hand of God, they will believe you when you talk to them about God, but when they see that your fears are greater than your faith, they may be more inclined to join the team that has the power to make you afraid.

Mothers, I want to suggest another area that you must address if you want to build self-esteem and dignity in your children. Be very careful of the way you talk about the fathers of your children and the men in their lives. Please stop running their dads down! You teach them to hate the part of themselves they receive from their dads when the only thing you have to say about their fathers is negative and belittling. You leave a door open for them to hate a part of you also when you are not fully honest with them about the role you played in the negativity of the broken relationship between you and their fathers. If you are going to tell them the negative things about their fathers or about the men in your life, at least tell them the positive things about them that caused you to fall in love with them or sleep with them. This will give them a chance to see that the male part of them that produced them was not all negative and unredeemable. Even if they were the product of rape or an abusive relationship, an understanding of what causes brokenness will give them a sense of balance so that they can see that even great positives can come out of negative situations and experiences.

Mothers, I know there is already a great demand on you for the well-being of your children, but I believe there is another doorway you can open to your sons and daughters which will allow them to see beyond what they see on television, YouTube, in their schools, or on their streets. You can open the world of spiritual and creative imagination to them by reading to them, having them read to you, and showing them how to try new and inventive things every day. You cannot teach them to fight their fears if you do not fight your own. You cannot let your depression overpower you and not expect the same depression to overpower them. Mothers, we need you to take up arms against fear. There are mothers working to make changes in our communities who have lost sons to gang violence, police violence, prison, and suicide. Mothers, I hope you will seek out their wisdom, which comes out of their pain, to save your sons and daughters and our communities from these tragic losses.

If you are the mother of a gang member, or if you are a gang member yourself, a great challenge is before you to do all of the above, and more, to turn the hearts and minds of the gang to become a force for good and not a force for evil. Ask God for wisdom as to how you can communicate with your own son and/or daughter as well as with their friends. Just the fact that you take the time to get to know their names and take time to talk to them, even if you do not approve of their lifestyle, can have an impact on their lives as well as the community. Show them how they can serve the elderly in the community, perhaps by improving their yards or at minimum just recognizing and respecting them. Help them put money on the accounts of their fellow soldiers who are in prison to show them they have not forgotten them. Help them to create an atmosphere of positive change and to become a positive force in the community. Help them learn to read and give them something powerful and positive to read that will change the atmosphere they bring to the gang, the streets, and their schools. Ask God to give you wisdom as to how you can communicate with the police and politicians so as not to undermine the strength, dignity, and self-esteem of the men and boys in your community, but send a message of willingness to communicate with anyone who truly has a heart to serve your community.

Secondly, I want to talk to the fathers. Unfortunately, as black men or men in any impoverished community where gang life is prevalent and the potential for violence is always present, there is a high level of anger and a high level of fear. We are more likely to be unemployed, profiled by law enforcement, imprisoned, killed, or labeled crazy. More than likely the women in our lives can read better and are employed better. Add children to that mix and a woman telling you that you are less than a man if you do not provide for her and for your children, and you have a volatile cocktail that explodes into domestic violence, child abuse, battered women, crime, imprisonment, death, and mental health disorders followed by medication. Whether you are a gang member, former gang member, worked all your life, abandoned your children, or are over your head in child support, it is time for us to ask the Most High for wisdom to educate ourselves and break the chokehold that is strangling our communities all over the world. When a man goes to war, he leaves home with the knowledge that he may die on the battlefield, but the best warriors fight as though they know they cannot lose.

Things have happened to us in life that have knocked us down and kept us down for a long time. Sometimes we have become bitter and angry and unable to see the possibility of winning. Some of us have gone through periods where laughter was not on the menu and we lost the hope of love from family and friends. Maybe you hurt others badly and did some things out of anger that you wish you could take back. No matter what situation we find ourselves in, or what situation we came out of, I believe God is calling us to battle. As men, dads, and fathers, our first battle is to restore our own hope so that we can restore the hope of our children, our families, and our communities. Our anger, hurt, and disappointment is killing the hope and laughter of our children. In order to win this battle for our souls and the souls of our children and loved ones, we are going to have to put ourselves on lockdown and discipline ourselves in new ways.

No matter how angry you become with your child's mother, her family, or society, determine in your heart and soul that you will be there for your child and that you will spend quality time with them when they have your undivided attention. Time spent with them will be more valuable than anything you can buy them. Make them laugh, tell your children stories, read to them, and ask them to read to you. They may lose what you buy them and forget it in the end, but they will cherish the laughter and the love you show them. They will always remember the stories you tell them, so tell them stories that give them hope and a future. In order to do this well, we have to take time to clear our heads of any anger we may have towards their moms or anyone else before we spend time with them because they will become poisoned by every negative vibe or spirit we bring to them. Draw on their positive energy and encourage them to love their mothers even if you do not get along with them. They will learn to respect women and themselves by the way you respect women and the way you respect yourself and others.

As men, we learn to be tough but we also have to learn how to be tender. Just as we pride ourselves on being tough and tender in making love, we must bring the same balance into the world to save our children, our families, and our communities. Even though we learn to be independent as men and boys, we cannot win this war by ourselves and neither can our children. They need us, even if we cannot afford to give them as much as we would like. They need to see the part of us that we hide from the world. Most of us would have done things differently in our lives if there had been more money in our families, more time spent with our parents, and more education at home and at school. Our social situations would be different if we grew up in drug-free, violence-free, and anger-free environments, but for most of us, this was not the case. All of these things affect the way we see the world, the way we raise our children, and the way we continue to live our lives. We tend to take out our anger over the conditions we grew up in on the women and children in our lives. Listen to them, love them, and ask God to help you understand them and their pain that comes from their environment and their own personal history, but do everything in your power never to hurt them because of your own pain or anger. As men, we must find a way to support each other and work together to create an environment in our communities where our women and children feel safe.

As men, fathers, and dads, one of the greatest things we can do for our children is to teach and show them by example how to treat women and people in general. Young boys and would-be thugs learn that women are simply for sex and money through their songs and the culture of the streets. Without meaningful work, constructive forms of discipline, and meaningful time spent with older men and women, there is nothing to keep the testosterone levels of young boys in balance. Without this balance, we have a recipe for disaster, which leads to sexual promiscuity and abuse, jealousy, gender confusion, murder, prison, death, and communities in chaos. As men, we must remember our mistakes and not judge the boys and young men for making the same mistakes or worse than we made, but we must find the patience and wisdom to help them overcome them faster than we did. It is not about beating them down but finding a way to build them up.

If you have not been in your children's lives and now realize the hurt and pain you have caused them, ask God for wisdom as to how you can begin to repair some of the damage. Do not expect them to receive you with open arms or hearts. Healing takes time. It can take years for any level of trust to be established, but please do not give up or become angry. Do the little things like calling, sending a card with heartfelt words or care and accountability. Spend three minutes, five minutes, thirty minutes, or whatever time feels right to build a relationship with them. Do not be too proud to let them know repeatedly, if necessary, that you have made mistakes, and that you want your future good to outweigh your past mistakes. There is too much at stake to let our pride get in the way of making these powerful contributions to the lives of our children and the future of our world.

I remember reading an article about juvenile delinquent elephants in a national park in South Africa. Years earlier the government decided to move wildlife to a reservation. The elephant population was too large and the larger male elephants were too large to move. They decided to kill the adult males, thinking that was a good solution. Years later, the young male elephants, with their testosterone out of control, were very aggressive with the female elephants and began attacking and killing rhinoceros. They formed into a gang and became so aggressive that the most aggressive juvenile elephant was shot and killed. After much research and money spent, the government decided to bring in older bull elephants from another location to see if it would help solve the problem. In just a short period, the behavior of the young male elephants changed towards the female elephants and the killing of rhinoceros stopped.

In similar fashion, our streets throughout the world have become reservations without strong, older male figures to teach and guide the young. If you do the research, you will find that the majority of men in prison and the majority of thugs on the streets have not had their fathers in their lives. We have to become fathers to the fatherless and better fathers to our own children. We must challenge ourselves and every other man to become powerful examples of men whose word is bond, and for whom truth, knowledge, and wisdom become our daily pursuit. We have to demonstrate the kind of power that does not rely on guns or physical prowess but an inner strength that guns and beat-downs cannot destroy or weaken. As young men see our strength, we give them a different model of a man, and we become new men in the process. We need them and they need us.

Chapter Ten

Calling Thugs and Saints

Because we are capable of communicating around the world faster and more effectively than ever before, we have the greatest potential to transform and heal the earth. If our lack of knowledge has been our reason for destroying our planet and ourselves, we now have access to more knowledge at our fingertips than ever with smart phones. Without knowledge of God, knowledge of ourselves, and wisdom, we are still destined to self-destruct with all of the knowledge we have at our fingertips. King Solomon said, "Wisdom is the principal thing; therefore get wisdom: and with all thy getting get understanding" (Proverbs 4:7). I have talked to thugs, I have talked to saints, and I believe there are thugs and saints who may not recognize that they are the same team, or at least could be. In the Hebrew Scriptures, before King David became king, his motley crew was a band of marauders made up of the discontented, the distressed, and those who were in debt (I Samuel 22:2). Together with the people, through reverence for God, they built a kingdom that served as a model for a kingdom ruled by God on earth. When David made important decisions for the nation, he asked God for direction. If we ask God for direction, I believe we may be surprised to see what can happen in our lives, our communities, and our world. We tried everything else, let us give it our best effort and see whether God will answer us.

I am not suggesting that calling upon God will be a quick fix to all of our problems. However, I am suggesting that it is possible for the nations and peoples of this world to call on the living God and receive answers that will transform our world. Many people have come to believe in God only after they have gone through some tremendous crisis and found that there was no way they could have survived without a miracle or some help greater than human help. With all of the anger, violence, hatred, and crime in our communities, we need God's help if we are going to make the world a better place and prepare it for the Kingdom of Heaven. We must call on God, and reverence God, but we must also put in work to make this happen, we must become the miracle.

This is where I make my appeal to both thugs and religious people all over the world because I believe the miracle takes place in conversations like the one I referred to earlier between the thug and the elderly woman in the church. We need dialogue, not diatribes, to bring about understanding in this world. It takes more courage to listen to someone with a heart to understand him or her than it does to judge them based on your own beliefs. It takes courage to communicate honestly and immediately. We need straight talk and transparency in order to heal the wounds in our world. Would a doctor prescribe medicine to a patient without talking to him or her? Would a doctor treat a patient without information about the patient's medical history? How can thugs judge the world as being against them without talking to someone on the other side to get an understanding of the bigger picture? How can religious people judge thugs or people of another religion without truly knowing them? How can people of one political party draw a line in the sand against another political party and say that their greatest concern is for the health and well-being of everyone in the nation? We definitely need a shift in thinking, but more importantly, we need a shift in our communication. We now have new towers of satellite communication that allow us to communicate worldwide, but the message will remain the same until our hearts change.

If more religious people like the elderly woman who was willing to die for what she believed could share with a caring heart, perhaps more hearts would change. Many of our heroes throughout history were former thugs who had divine encounters that changed their lives and often because someone took the time to listen or talk to them. Even today, there are thugs on earth who have had divine encounters and who now recognize and reverence God. There are religious people who, in their zeal for God became judgmental but remembered how love and grace change and are now helping others to change by living a life that gives what they received. There are disciplined, trained, and dedicated soldiers whom God has prepared in every nation, who are ready at a moment's notice to demonstrate the power of love, forgiveness, and sound judgment.

A twenty-one-year-old white male, indoctrinated with hate messages, enters a black church in Charleston, South Carolina, shoots, and kills nine parishioners during a Bible study. A different scenario than the one painted earlier in this book, but one that created dialogue between people across lines drawn in the sand. While it is true that the confederate flag represents one thing to one part of the community and another thing to another part, the flag itself is not the heart of the problem. As confederate flags disappear from state houses, as the wearing of gang flags and colors become illegal in schools and courtrooms, and as symbols of violence and hatred disappear from public view, the problem will persist until hearts are changed. There is no doubt that our earth is under siege and that we are at war against an evil that threatens to destroy humanity. In a time of war that threatens a nation or a people, every person plays a role in the defense of the nation. Until we make the sacrifice to understand one another, the prisons, psych wards, and cemeteries are going to continue to overflow with wasted gifts and talents and lives lost prematurely.

Everyone can play a role in preparing the way for the Kingdom of God to come on earth because the Kingdom of God comes with a change of heart. God said through the prophet Ezekiel, "A new heart also will I give you, and a new spirit will I put within you: and I will take away the stony heart out of your flesh, and I will give you a heart of flesh" (Ezekiel 36:26). The portal that allows the Kingdom of God to come to earth is the human heart. When the heart changes, the world changes. Thugs, saints, and religious people of all faiths can rend their hearts in recognition of the fact that everyone makes mistakes and needs to be forgiven, maybe some more than others. This means that everyone can play a role in changing the atmosphere of earth, even those who are in prison, the handicapped, the abused, children, the elderly, thugs, saints, religious people of all faiths, and even atheists and agnostics.

If you are a thug, your greatest act of courage will be converting all of the energy and dedication you gave to taking from others into giving to others. The gifts and talents you used for evil, determine in your mind and heart to use them for good. Where lying was your way of life, make honesty with wisdom your new way of life. Take full responsibility for your past actions and endure the judgment of people, but write a new story with the rest of your life. Instead of beating soldiers down to enter your ranks to follow your orders, train them to rule themselves and to follow God's orders. Our greatest fight is spiritual, so remember that our war is not with people, our war is for people. Our war is with those spirits that cause us to do wrong and keep us prisoner to fear, anger, hatred, and violence. If we defeat the spirits, we can save the people. No one can defeat a spirit better than the one who knows that spirit. As you conquer the spirits in you, your example of strength will inspire others to do the same, and the Kingdom of Heaven will get stronger on earth.

As in every war, there will be casualties, but be as strong to die for the Kingdom of Heaven as you were to die for turf and pride.

If you are in prison, use the same network you use to keep in touch with and control the outside world to change the atmosphere inside and outside of the prison walls. As you already know the power and influence those in prison have on the streets, your strength and influence can be just as great as a force to build the community. Your greatest risk to life will come as you break down the divisions of race, religion, gang affiliation, and turf inside the prison walls. In doing so, you not only upset the power structure inside the prison but outside as well. As the spirit of God transforms you, and you begin to transform the environment and atmosphere of the prison, some will die, but for everyone that dies, like Stephen in the biblical book of Acts, ten more will rise. Every justice system throughout the world will feel the impact of your commitment to die for the Kingdom of Heaven. As you ask God for wisdom and common sense, you will receive the strength and courage needed to make your greatest contribution to the new heaven and the new earth.

Whether you are a spiritual person or a religious person, the greatest contribution you can make to the Kingdom of Heaven is "to do justly, and to love mercy, and to walk humbly with your God" (Micah 6:8). It is not the defense of our religions or our beliefs that will change the world but the demonstration of them. I would like to take the liberty to change the characters in the parable of Jesus about the Good Samaritan. It was not the Christian, the Jew, the Muslim, the New Ager, or any other religious or political personality that changed the man's plight. It was the one who risked his own life and reputation to help a person in need. Therefore, this cry and this call goes to all saints and to all who believe in a Most High God.

A woman brought to Jesus had been caught committing adultery. The Mosaic Law said that both the man and the woman were to be stoned to death. The religious people were ready to stone her when Jesus said, "He that is without sin among you, let him first cast a stone at her." When they all walked away, Jesus told her that he did not condemn her and he set her free, telling her to live a changed life (John 8:7-12). We are the gatekeepers of the kingdom of God, and we can free others by refusing to condemn them just as Jesus did for this woman. Surely, someone reading this will look for another scripture that will condemn the person anyway, but someone knows how his or her life changed by this kind of forgiveness. As the spirit of judgment and condemnation is conquered, more people young and old will experience the power and freedom of the Kingdom of God.

I read or heard once, the account of someone who had a vision of heaven and hell. In the vision, the person was ushered to hell where he saw a long table beautifully set and supplied with a heavenly looking meal, with the best meats, breads, vegetables, and beverages, before souls seated on both sides of the table. The souls were tormented and in misery because they could not access the food on the table. The person seeing this vision saw no barrier to prohibit the souls from accessing the food. However, upon closer inspection, he noticed that the eating and serving utensils at the table extended from one side of the table to the other so that no one could feed or serve themselves. Because they could not die in hell, they were destined to live in the presence of plenty but be unable to enjoy it. Immediately, the person was ushered to heaven where he observed the exact scenario with what appeared to be the same long table beautifully set and supplied with a heavenly looking meal with the best meats, breads, vegetables, and beverages set before souls seated on both sides of the table. Even the eating and serving utensils at the table extended from one side of the table to the other, the same as in hell, so that no one could feed or serve themselves. In heaven, however, the souls were laughing and enjoying themselves. Upon closer observation, the person seeing the vision noticed that, although they could not serve or feed themselves in heaven, they were happily serving and feeding each other.

As in the vision, living selfishly and separated from one another, we create the atmosphere of hell on earth. We have the power to create the atmosphere of heaven around us when we learn to share and help one another. Gangs form and members join for self-preservation, but in the Kingdom of Heaven we forgive to redeem others, we share to relieve others, and we work to release others. As thugs and saints catch the Spirit of the Kingdom of Heaven, we will use our shared resources to create opportunities for self-employment to keep our young men and women legally and gainfully employed. We will create an atmosphere where forgiveness can restore lives and where wisdom is more valuable than money and possessions. The goal in the Kingdom of Heaven is to neither govern, nor be governed by other human beings. Our hearts governed by the spirit and wisdom of God grant us the privilege of having God as our banner over us. Then we are truly free indeed.

> "Our Father in heaven,
> hallowed be your name,
> your kingdom come,
> your will be done,
> on earth as it is in heaven.
> Give us today our daily bread.
> And forgive us our debts,
> as we also have forgiven our debtors.
> And lead us not into temptation,
> but deliver us from the evil one."

CPSIA information can be obtained
at www.ICGtesting.com
Printed in the USA
FFOW03n1903240116
20609FF